SEVEN SECONDS TO DIE

SEVEN SECONDS
TO DIE

A Military Analysis of the Second Nagorno-Karabakh War
and the Future of Warfighting

JOHN ANTAL

CASEMATE

Philadelphia & Oxford

Published in the United States of America and Great Britain in 2022 by
CASEMATE PUBLISHERS
1950 Lawrence Road, Havertown, PA 19083, USA
and
The Old Music Hall, 106–108 Cowley Road, Oxford OX4 1JE, UK

Paperback Edition: ISBN 978-1-63624-123-4
Digital Edition: ISBN 978-1-63624-124-1

A CIP record for this book is available from the British Library

Printed and bound in the United States of America by Integrated Books International

Typeset in India by Lapiz Digital Services, Chennai.

For a complete list of Casemate titles, please contact:

CASEMATE PUBLISHERS (US)
Telephone (610) 853-9131
Fax (610) 853-9146
Email: casemate@casematepublishers.com
www.casematepublishers.com

CASEMATE PUBLISHERS (UK)
Telephone (01865) 241249
Email: casemate-uk@casematepublishers.co.uk
www.casematepublishers.co.uk

Cover image credit: istockphoto / Julia Garan

Contents

Foreword

Learn and adapt, or lose to those who do. This is the hard calculus of war. Capable people die when they ignore the reality of the modern battlespace, and the reality of modern war is changing ever faster as the methods of war continuously evolve with the advance of technology.

The Second Nagorno-Karabakh War, which occurred from September 27 to November 10, 2020, is a war that military and national security professionals must study. This war was one of historic watersheds in military technology and methods of war. It was the first war in history that was shaped and primarily won by robotic systems. To be sure, machines did not win this war alone. The teaming of human soldiers with the effects of unmanned systems was crucial.

The lessons of this war provide a glimpse of wars to come. As author John Antal emphasizes in this book, those involved in national defense have an obligation to study recent wars, derive lessons, and turn these into action. In this effort, time is vital as lessons applied too late to make a difference become irrelevant. Acting in time, before an adversary can use the changing methods of warfare to their advantage against you, is what we expect from those shouldered with the responsibility of our defense. Failure in this arena ends badly for everyone, whereas success can deter war or win it.

The author, Colonel John Antal, US Army (Retired), is uniquely qualified to bring the lessons of the Second Nagorno-Karabakh War to the reader. Colonel Antal has conducted a detailed analysis of the Second Nagorno-Karabakh War and spent the past year briefing senior government and military decision-makers about the war and raising the alarm. He has completed his comprehensive and well-written review using a broad range of open-source information and applying his keen sense of military operations and military history to the effort. His study is a wake-up call that highlights the changing methods of war that government and military professionals should heed.

Decisive wars are uncommon. In the Second Nagorno-Karabakh War, Azerbaijan waged a modern military campaign in multiple domains that resulted in the decisive defeat of Armenia in 44 days. Armenia fought bravely, but was neither trained nor equipped for the modern war unleashed by Azerbaijan. Azerbaijan over-matched Armenia at nearly every level. Azerbaijan, with extensive help from Turkey, unleashed a force of unmanned aerial systems and loitering munitions that disintegrated the Armenian air defense network, secured air supremacy, and then set about destroying command and control, artillery, tanks, armored vehicles and personnel. It took soldiers working closely with these unmanned systems to finish the war, but the smart use of unmanned systems, at a scale not seen before, shaped the campaign. We should learn from this decisive war, understand its lessons, and use this knowledge to prepare for coming storms.

Dr Alexander Kott
Army Research Laboratory
Alexander Kott

Acknowledgements

This book deals with an important and unpleasant subject: preparing for the next war. Writing a book that will impel people to think and act on this subject is about starting a dialogue—a cooperative two-war conversation—and sharing that dialogue with the world. Creating a compelling dialogue requires the support of many people. This work is totally my own and not the work of any government organization or group. All information for this book was drawn from open-source information. I wish to thank those who helped transform *Seven Seconds to Die* from a thought to publication. First, a very special thanks to my amazing wife, Uncha Antal. She inspires me every day and makes all things possible. Second, I want to thank Dr. Alexander Kott for writing the foreword to this book and engaging in our discussions about the events and lessons of the Second Nagorno Karabakh War. Next, I want to thank Colonel (Retired) Francis Fierko and Colonel (Retired) Rick Jung, for taking time to discuss, analyze and review the manuscript. Their editorial help and keen insight were crucial. I also want to thank Shawn Graves and Carolyn Petracca for their comments and advice. Finally, I am thankful for the editing and advice of the manuscript from Andy Wright and Ruth Sheppard of Casemate Publishers. I am eternally thankful to all of you.

Names Used in this Book for Locations, Villages, Towns and Cities in Nagorno-Karabakh

Armenian and Azerbaijani names for locations, villages, towns and cities in Nagorno-Karabakh and the surrounding regions are sometimes different. Stepanakert, the capital of Armenian Nagorno-Karabakh, is called Khankendi by the Azerbaijanis. This can become very confusing and writing multiple names for each location is tedious. My method is to use the name of the nation that owned the area after the November 10, 2020, ceasefire. I have therefore decided to use the following names throughout this book for the locations listed below. Some of these use the Armenian name and some the Azerbaijani. The names of locations used in this book are listed here in alphabetical order in the left column of the table below, along with their Armenian and Azerbaijani equivalents.

Location Name Used	Armenian	Azerbaijani
Agdam	Aghdam	Agdam
Dashalty	Karin Tak	Dasalti/Dashalty
Fazuli	Fizuli	Fazuli
Goris	Goris	Goris
Hadrut	Hadrat	Hadrut
Horadiz Passage	Horadiz	Horadiz
Jabril	Jabril	Jabril
Lachin		Lachin
Madagiz	Madagiz	Sugovushan
Shusha	Shushi	Shusha
Stepanakert	Stepanakert	Khankendi

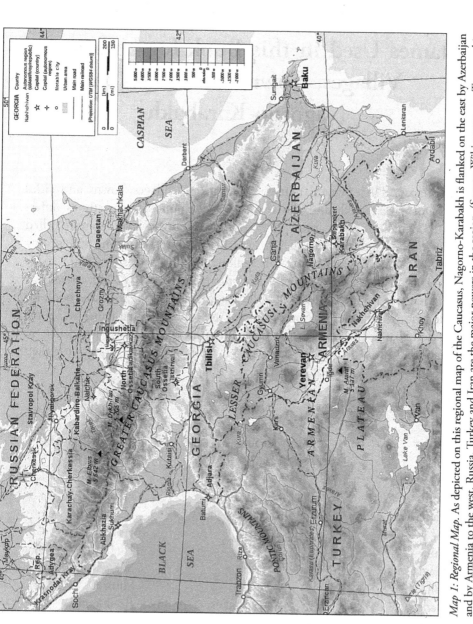

Map 1: Regional Map. As depicted on this regional map of the Caucasus, Nagorno-Karabakh is flanked on the east by Azerbaijan and by Armenia to the west. Russia, Turkey and Iran are the major powers in the region. (Source: Wiki commons, Topographic data from the NASA Shuttle Radar Topography Mission)

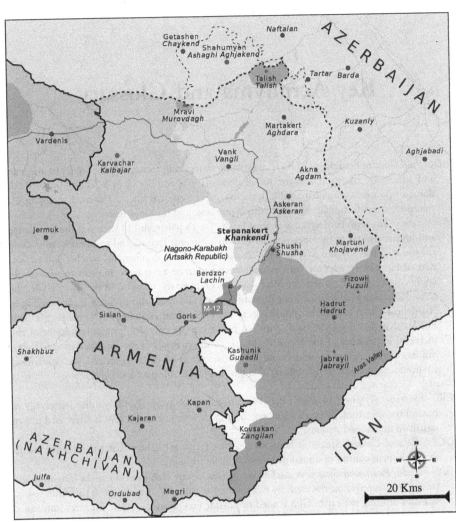

Map 2: Key Towns in Nagorno-Karabakh. This map depicts the key towns and the road from Goris–Lachin–Shusha–Stepanakert (near the center of the map), known as the Lachin corridor, in the Nagorno-Karabakh battle area. The dark dotted line is the original Line of Control, before the war began, and the light dotted line marks territory Artsakh claims but Azerbaijan controlled before the war. Azerbaijan took the territory in the darkest shade from Artsakh during the war and other areas were ceded after the ceasefire. Russian peacekeeping troops were stationed in the remaining Artsakh territory to guard the Lachin corridor connecting Armenia and Artsakh. (Source: adapted from Wiki commons)

Key Acronyms and Glossary

ADO   All Domain Operations: ADO is an evolving warfighting concept for the ability to integrate and effectively command and control all domains in a conflict or in a crisis seamlessly. All domain operations use global capabilities: space, cyber, deterrent (the nuclear triad, for example), transportation, electromagnetic spectrum operations, and missile defense.

Battlespace: The term battlespace is defined by the US Department of Defense as the knowledge and understanding of the operational area's environment, factors, and conditions, to include the status of friendly and adversary forces, neutrals and non-combatants, weather and terrain, that enables timely, relevant, comprehensive, and accurate assessments in order to successfully apply combat power, protect the force, and/or complete the mission. In the past decade, the term battlespace transformed from primarily a time and space-driven linear understanding (a "battlefield") to a multidimensional system of systems understanding (a "battlespace"). This implies that managing the battlespace has become more complex, primarily because of the increased importance of the cognitive domain, a direct result of the information age. Today, militaries are expected to understand all of the effects of their actions on the operational environment, not just in the military domain (land, sea, air, space and cyber).

Drone: Unmanned aerial vehicle.

EW   Electronic Warfare: The use of the electromagnetic spectrum (EMS), or directed energy to control the spectrum, to attack an enemy or impede enemy assaults. EW is often used to jam signals to unmanned systems.

GCS   Ground Control System: a land- or sea-based control center that provides the facilities for human control of unmanned aerial vehicles (drones).

GPS   Global Positioning System: A satellite navigation system that determines the longitude and latitude of a receiver on the earth by calculating the time difference from signals from several satellites orbiting the earth. GPS is used to provide geo-positioning data for most unmanned aerial systems.

HITL   Human In The Loop: Weapon system that, once activated, is intended to only engage individual targets or specific target groups that have been selected by a human operator. Includes "Fire and Forget" munitions.

HOTL   Human On The Loop: An autonomous weapon system that is designed to provide human operators with the ability to intervene and terminate engagements, including in the event of a weapon system failure, before unacceptable levels of damage occur.

HOOTL Human Out Of The Loop: A weapon system that, once activated, can select and engage targets without further intervention by a human operator.

IOBT Internet of Battlefield Things: The Internet of Battlefield Things is an emerging capability that will connect soldiers with smart technology in armor, radios, weapons, and other objects, to give troops "extra sensory" perception, offer situational understanding, endow fighters with prediction powers, provide better risk assessment, and develop shared intuitions.

JADO   Joint All Domain Operations: JADO is an evolution of the concept of multi-domain operations (MDO). JADO incorporates the massive potential of a truly integrated force (the focus of MDO) and updates the concept by incorporating joint and combined aspects for the conduct of future operations.

Kill Chain: A cross-domain military targeting construct that connects sensors, shooters, and command-and-control nodes. The sequential operations of a kill chain are to identify the target; track; decide to strike the target; dispatch the force to the target; destroy the target; assess the effects; if effects are unsatisfactory, reinitiate the sequence. A kill chain operates at human decision-making speeds and at multiple echelons of command, using a human in the loop command-and-control hierarchy. An example of a kill chain is the use of a human-controlled MQ-9 Reaper, armed with Hellfire missiles, to destroy a high-value target.

Kill Web: An emerging concept for a multidomain warfighting network that leverages artificial intelligence to synchronize the internet of battlefield things to deliver desired effects in real-time. A kill web operates at artificial intelligence speeds with human on the loop or human out of the loop oversight. A "micro" example of a kill web is the network that targets, tracks, and fires the MK 15 Phalanx to defend ships and fixed points. Once realized, the emerging kill web concept will connect with every sensor and shooter in a designated battlespace and, once given targeting parameters, execute strike operations at artificial intelligence and machine speeds.

LM   Loitering Munition: A category of weapons that are a persistent form of precision fires. A loitering munition (also known as a kamikaze or suicide) loiters above a designated area until it identifies a target. The LM then attacks the target by crashing into it. LMs enable faster kill chain reaction times. They can be controlled or operate autonomously. The Israel Aerospace Industries-produced Harop is an example of an LM that can operate and function autonomously, searching and launching attacks without human intervention.

LRPF   Long-Range Precision Fires: Precision-guided munitions, launched from land, sea or air, that, when connected into a sensor network, have both long range and accuracy.

MDO   Multi-Domain Operations: MDO describes how the US Army, as part of the joint force (Army, Navy, Air Force, and Marines) can counter and defeat a near-peer adversary capable of contesting the US in all domains (air, land, maritime, space, and cyberspace) in both competition and armed conflict.

MLRS   Multiple Launch Rocket System: A rocket launching platform that can rapidly fire many rockets.

sUAS   Small Unmanned Aerial System: Small unmanned aircraft that weigh under twenty pounds, have a ceiling of 1,200 feet above ground level and fly at speeds less than 100 knots (115mph).

UAS   Unmanned Aerial System: Also called unmanned aircraft system. The term UAS represents the entire package of components that include the unmanned aerial vehicle and the ground control system, and the necessary equipment, network, and personnel to control an unmanned aircraft.

UAV   Unmanned Aerial Vehicle: an unmanned aerial vehicle, commonly called a drone, is an unmanned aircraft. UAVs are the flying component of an unmanned aerial system.

UCAV Unmanned Combat Aerial Vehicle: an unmanned combat aerial vehicle is an unmanned aerial vehicle that is used for intelligence, surveillance, target acquisition, and reconnaissance and carries ordnance such as anti-tank guided missiles, and/or bombs on hardpoints for drone strikes.

The Second Nagorno-Karabakh War saw the "coming of age" of loitering munitions in the modern battlespace and provided important lessons in the use of unmanned aerial systems and precision fires in modern war. The methods of warfare are changing rapidly and militaries around the globe are racing to keep up. In this photo, the US military tests the launch of an Altius 600 loitering munition from an Advanced Ground Off-Road tactical ground vehicle. The multipurpose Altius 600, produced by California-based defense technology firm Anduril Industries, has a range of 440 kilometers (273 miles), can operate at a ceiling of 25,000 feet and provides intelligence, surveillance and reconnaissance, signals intelligence information, counter unmanned aerial systems effects, and precision strike capability against ground targets. In July 2021, the US Department of Defense awarded a five-year US$99 million contract to Anduril Industries for the purchase of its counter-drone system. Many systems such as the Altius will use artificial intelligence to operate with increasing autonomy in the coming years. (US Army photo)

Why the Second Nagorno-Karabakh War is Important

"War is a matter of speed—speed in decision, action, and coordination—and speed wins war. Speed is the most powerful weapon of war. *Speeding up the Kill Chain is the essence of modern war.*"

COLONEL JOHN ANTAL, US ARMY, RETIRED,
IN AN ADDRESS TO THE US ARMY FIRES COMMAND CENTER OF EXCELLENCE,
AT FORT SILL, OKLAHOMA, SEPTEMBER 2, 2021

Foresight is a human quality in great demand today. Foresight is the ability to fix problems in the short term and develop solutions for the long run. We need leaders with foresight in our rapidly changing world. We particularly need leaders who can execute foresight in military affairs. Warfare consists of both principles and methods. Today, we desperately require leaders with the foresight to understand the unchanging principles of war and the ever-changing methods of war. "If you learn only methods," Ralph Waldo Emerson once famously said, "you'll be tied to your methods. But if you learn principles, you can devise your own methods." Methods are many and always change. Principles are few and remain constant. This is the difference between a chef and a cook. The cook wants the recipe and knows only the methods. The chef understands the principles and masters the methods to create something new and amazing. In short, the chef has mastered the recipe to make a meal for one person or can create a culinary delight for a huge multicourse banquet. Expert chefs develop foresight.

War is a timeless paradox. While its principles remain unchanged, its goals, ways and means are constantly evolving, requiring practitioners to study the changing methods to improve, upgrade, and prepare for the next conflict, or risk ignominious defeat. The principles of war outlined by Sun Tzu, the ancient Chinese author of the *Art of War* written around the 5th century BC, are as relevant today in the information age as when war was waged with muscle power, spears and swords. The principles of strategy, operational art, and tactics of the Peloponnesian War, for example, fought between Athens and Sparta (431–405 BC), can also provide insights for current conflicts despite a myriad of conditions, not the least of which is technology, forcing means and methods to constantly change and adapt.

The changing methods of war

Today, the means of warfare, often referred to as the methods of war, are changing fast. Exponential technological growth in computing power and the microminiaturization of components is accelerating this trend. Keeping up with the changing methods of war requires focus and study.

War is the use of violence to achieve some purpose through a correlation of goals, ways, and means. According to Carl von Clausewitz, "… war is not merely an act of policy but a true political instrument, a continuation of political intercourse, carried on with other means … The political object is the goal, war is the means of reaching it, and means can never be considered in isolation from their purpose."[1] Today, the means of warfare, often referred to as the methods of war, are changing fast. Exponential technological growth in computing power and the microminiaturization of components is accelerating this trend. Keeping up with the changing methods of war requires focus and study. To understand how these exponential developments impact the changing methods of war requires study in breadth and depth. Recent conflicts can provide vital insights and are, therefore, important to examine. The Second Nagorno-Karabakh War that occurred in the second half of 2020 is such a conflict and a pivotal event worthy of investigation. This war requires in-depth study by military professionals and those involved in national defense. We ignore this war, and the lessons we can derive from it, at our peril.

From late September 2020, in the mountainous region of the Caucasus called Nagorno-Karabakh, a war was fought between Azerbaijan and Armenia that provided a glimpse of conflicts to come. This was not only a war between medium powers with fully developed military forces, it was also a decisive military conflict. It resulted in a complete military victory for Azerbaijan. Decisive wars are rare. In 44 days, Azerbaijan conducted a multidimensional military campaign that ended in an indisputable military victory against a near equally matched foe holding defensive positions in mountainous terrain. Conducted amid the worldwide Covid-19 pandemic, and during the run-up to a major presidential election in the United States which held the focus of much of the world, few people in the west paid attention to this far-off conflict. This is unfortunate, for the war waged in Nagorno-Karabakh was a watershed.

The Second Nagorno-Karabakh War was the first war in history won primarily by robotic systems. It is a dramatic harbinger of the dawn of unmanned, intelligent machine warfare.

The Second Nagorno-Karabakh War in 2020

The first war in history won primarily by robotic systems.

The title of this book, *Seven Seconds to Die,* was derived from a comment made by an anonymous Armenian soldier who said that, when they heard the enemy's Israeli-made Harop loitering munitions flying overhead, they had seven seconds to run or die. Seven seconds is a remarkably short time for a semi-autonomous weapon system to identify the target, verify a match with its targeting parameters, and strike. Speed is the essential element of war as speed wins time. Time is equal to all sides. The combatant that wins time, wins the battle. In a war where unmanned systems can find and then strike in seven seconds, and the opponent can do nothing but run or die, the side with this capability gains a tremendous physical and morale advantage. Throughout the battlespace, Armenian tanks, air defense systems, artillery, command posts, and soldiers were hit and destroyed by top-attack munitions, many of them autonomous. For the Armenians, whose air defense was either destroyed or ineffective, there was no way to stop the attackers. It did not matter if their positions were camouflaged or not. It did not matter if they were moving or stationary, or whether it was day or night. When they rushed inside their bunkers for protection, the loitering munitions would follow them into the entrance and explode. There was no rest and no safe places. The Armenians had nowhere to hide and nowhere to run. They could not mask from the enemy's machines; they were slaughtered at machine speeds.

Asking tough questions is the key to gaining insight. Answering those questions is the key to developing foresight. *Seven Seconds to Die* identifies key combat trends from a careful study of the Second Nagorno-Karabakh War and then uses those changing methods to generate questions relevant to the development of military technology and war. These questions also provide the elements for the creation of case studies to test future concepts in thought experiments, wargames, and simulations against a full spectrum of military threats. It seems self-evident that if we ignore the lessons of the Second Nagorno-Karabakh War, and assume through hubris or cultural bias that this conflict is not worthy of our study, we will pay for our ignorance in blood and treasure. Learning from other conflicts is the most effectual means of gaining insights at low cost and without risk. It is the key to choosing either technological stagnation or breakthrough, blindness or foresight.

Learning from other conflicts

It seems self-evident that if we ignore the lessons of the Second Nagorno-Karabakh War, and assume through hubris or cultural bias that this conflict is not worthy of our study, we will pay for our ignorance in blood and treasure. Learning from other conflicts is the most effectual means of gaining insights at low cost and without risk.

Seven Seconds to Die is a book that uses open-source information about the Second Nagorno-Karabakh War to discover lessons that have applicability to future military operations. This book uses the conflict as a jumping-off point to peer into the future of warfare. Every war has its unique elements and any system that generates an advantage in one conflict can be countered in the next. Not studying how this was won, however, almost guarantees those unheeded lessons will have to be relearned in blood in the next conflict. Learning these lessons and preparing in time to deter or win the next conflict is what is at stake.

War is changing and the Second Nagorno-Karabakh War offers vital insights into the nature of multi-domain combat. The object of war, as explained by Sun Tzu, Thucydides, and Clausewitz, is the submission of the enemy as quickly and efficiently as possible and is intended to advance political objectives. Azerbaijan achieved its political objectives by waging a decisive military campaign using new methods of war and timeless principles. The methods of warfare used in the Second Nagorno-Karabakh War should not be overestimated or underestimated. The war did not usher in an era that ended combined arms operations, nor did it announce the death of the tank. It does, however, provide a glimpse into unmanned systems combat as no other conflict ever has. The lessons from this war are, therefore, instructive and prescient. Military professionals, government leaders, and informed citizens should be aware of these lessons, contemplate their significance, and take appropriate action. We need leaders with foresight. The intent of this book is to assist you in that journey.

John Antal
September 2021

This image is a frame from a real-time video feed from an Azerbaijani loitering munition that is recording strikes on Armenian D-20 Howitzers. The drone in this strike is an Israeli-made Orbiter 1K unmanned aerial system. A second loitering munition, at the top left of the image, flies past the explosion to strike another howitzer. Orbiter 1Ks attacked and destroyed all six guns of the artillery battery in less than five minutes. The Orbiter 1K independently scans the battle area and automatically detects and destroys stationary or moving targets. If the loitering munition does not observe a target, it will search the battlespace until it does. Once a target fits its predesignated parameters, it dives into the target and explodes. If it does not observe a target, the Orbiter 1K will fly to a predesignated area before it runs out of fuel. Arriving at the landing area, it then falls to the ground by parachute and airbag to allow for reuse. The CP Aeronautics Orbiter 1K is a catapult-launched loitering munition that carries a 3-kilogram (6.6lb) warhead, has a range of 100 kilometers (60 miles), and an endurance of 2.5 hours. (Image capture from Azerbaijani Ministry of Defense video).

CHAPTER I

Preparation for War

"It is better to be wise after the event than not wise at all, and wisdom after one event may lead to wisdom before another."

SIR JOHN C. SLESSOR, *AIR POWER AND ARMIES*

There is a Russian saying that applies to the Caucasus: "Two bears don't live in one lair." An American version of this might be: "This town ain't big enough for the both of us." This was the crux of the problem between Christian Armenia and Muslim Azerbaijan in 1988 as the Soviet Union dissolved. Armenians and Azerbaijanis both coveted the same lair, Nagorno-Karabakh. They called most of the same places by different, culturally possessive names, and they were willing to kill to own it.

Nagorno-Karabakh is a land-locked, kidney bean-shaped mountainous region situated between Armenia and Azerbaijan in the southern Caucasus. In Persian, "kara" means "dark" or "black" and "bak/bagh" refers to garden; so, "black garden". In Russian, Нагорный Карабах (Nagorno-Karabakh) translates as "Mountainous Karabakh." The area was named the "Republic of Artsakh" by Armenians after the first war, as Artsakh was the original name of the ancient Armenian Kingdom's 10th province. The Nagorno-Karabakh mountains dominate the Aras Valley to the south and southeast and overlook the lower ground to the east that runs to Baku, the capital of Azerbaijan. Most of this mountainous terrain is 950 meters (3,120 feet) above sea level. Considered by many as the heart of the south Caucasus, the region is roughly 4,400 square kilometers (1,700 square miles) in area, about the size of the US state of Delaware, or twice the size of the US Army's National Training Center at Fort Irwin, California. There are grass-covered steppes in the lowlands and thick forests of oak, beech, birch, and hornbeam in the higher elevations. Nearly 36 percent of Nagorno-Karabakh is covered in forest. The area is also dotted with ancient and holy religious sites, most dating back to the

Middle Ages. Some of these, like the fortress in Shusha, still offer formidable protection from small arms and mortar fire. The weather is moderate until winter, from mid-November until April, when it turns cold with heavy fog and frequent snowfalls. From a military point of view, the high ground in Nagorno-Karabakh favors the defense. For an attacker, the best time to seize the critical terrain and mountain passes is before winter sets in and makes movement in the higher elevations difficult.

The distance from Stepanakert (the capital of Armenian-controlled Nagorno-Karabakh) to Baku (the capital of Azerbaijan) is roughly 274 kilometers (170 miles). The distance from Stepanakert to Yerevan (the capital of Armenia) is about 195 kilometers (121 miles). Roads are key to traversing mountain regions and military movement through the Nagorno-Karabakh mountains can be blocked by controlling key passes and chokepoints. "The immediate objective of a mountainous defense is to deny the enemy access to key terrain that helps him conduct further operations. Therefore, it is necessary to defend in terrain that restricts and contains the enemy, as well as control the high ground that dominates this terrain."[2] Narrow, winding roads up steep mountains provide the defender with many opportunities to ambush an attacker. The road network in the mountainous Nagorno-Karabakh area is largely undeveloped and movement though the mountains is slow, difficult, and dangerous to an attacking army. Other than foot-trails through the mountains, the only major, modern road in Nagorno-Karabakh is the M-12 Highway that runs from Goris, traversing the narrow Lachin corridor to connect Lachin, Shusha, and Stepanakert. Control of the highway is key to controlling Nagorno-Karabakh.

The US Army defines "key terrain" as "any locality, or area, the seizure or retention of which affords a marked advantage to either combatant." The US Army further defines "decisive terrain" as key terrain whose seizure and retention are mandatory to accomplish the mission. Decisive terrain is relatively rare and it may not be present in every military situation. There can be several areas of key terrain, but there should only be one piece of decisive terrain in a battle area. "In the mountains, more so than in the lowlands, the strength of the defense depends on its selection and use of key and decisive terrain. Key and decisive terrain provides the defender—and usually denies the attacker—excellent observation and fighting positions."[3] The key terrain in Nagorno-Karabakh, therefore, consists primarily of five areas: The Horadiz passage, the town of Hadrut, the Lachin corridor, the city of Shusha, and the capital city of Stepanakert.

The Horadiz passage is a narrow passage 10–12 kilometers (6–7 miles) wide along the Aras/Araks/Araxes River. This passage leads to the Geyan steppe and, to the north, roads that lead to the M-12 Highway that connects Lachin–Shusha–Stepanaert. To move along the Nagorno-Karabakh/Iranian border and avoid a direct assault up steep mountains, you must control, and move through, the Horadiz passage and then the Aras Valley. For the Azerbaijanis, controlling the Aras Valley was vital as it is the only way to approach the M-12 Highway, Shusha and Stepanakert without a direct east-to-west mountain assault. Once into the Aras Valley, any attacking force has room to disperse and maneuver. If the Armenians interdicted the Horadiz passage, with artillery or air forces, they could inflict heavy casualties on any Azerbaijani forces moving through.

Hadrut is a village and a regional center, with an Armenian population of less than 4,000 inhabitants (in 2020), that controls the road to the center of Nagorno-Karabakh and the cities of Shusha and Stepanakert. The largest city in Nagorno-Karabakh is Stepanakert and has an Armenian population of approximately 75,000.

The Lachin corridor connecting Nagorno-Karabakh with Armenia is also key terrain, the two-lane M-12 being the only major road. The corridor is easy to defend as there are many places to establish roadblocks and ambushes. Attacking up the corridor can be a challenge for a mechanized-armored force. If you control the Lachin corridor with enough anti-tank guided missile units supported by artillery, you can establish a robust defense. If you control the corridor, then you control everything that comes by road into and out of Nagorno-Karabakh.

Shusha, and ten nearby villages, is in the center of Nagorno-Karabakh and is the decisive military terrain. The city overlooks the city of Stepanakert, sitting on a plateau that forms a natural fortress with steep cliffs. Shusha sits on this high ground, south of Stepanakert, only 15 kilometers (9 miles) away by road. More importantly, the straight-line distance from Shusha to Stepanakert, and therefore the distance for artillery and missiles to range, is only four kilometers (2.5 miles). He who holds Shusha gains a tremendous, war-winning advantage.

Stepanakert, the city with the largest population of any urban area in Nagorno-Karabakh, is key terrain as threatening, or seizing, it would provide a marked military and political advantage to Azerbaijan. It is unknown if Azerbaijan's general staff ever seriously considered fighting for Stepanakert, but if they seized Shusha, there would be little need to do so.

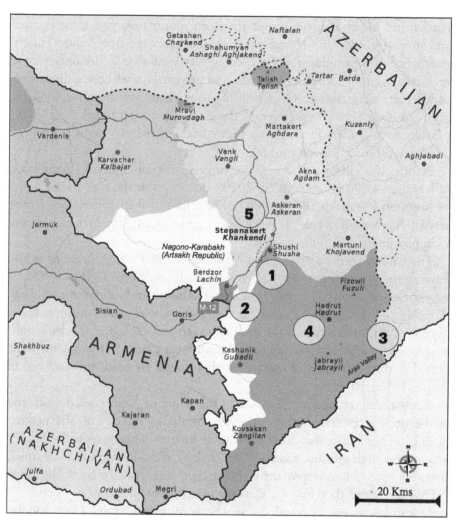

Map 3: Key Terrain in Nagorno-Karabakh. The key terrain is shown on this map (compare with Map 1), in order from east to west to north: 1. Horadiz passage into the Aras Valley; 2. Hadrut; 3. Lachin corridor; 4. Shusha (decisive terrain); and 5. Stepanakert. (Source: adapted from Wiki commons)

The First Nagorno-Karabakh War 1988–1994

The First Nagorno-Karabakh War was fought between hastily organized Armenian and Azerbaijani forces using Soviet-era equipment and tactics. Armenia, the victor, suffered nearly 30,000 civilian and military casualties. Azerbaijan, the loser, lost up to 80,000 civilians and military personnel killed or wounded. Hundreds of thousands of civilians were displaced on both sides as Armenians occupied their territorial gains after this hard-fought conflict.

Since of the end of World War I, Armenians and Azerbaijanis have been at each other's throats. The *casus belli* for the First Nagorno-Karabakh War, fought from February 20, 1988, to May 12, 1994, was the combination of decades of hatred between the Armenians and Azerbaijanis over a decision made by Soviet dictator Joseph Stalin in 1921 to designate the region as a part of the Soviet Socialist Republic of Azerbaijan rather than the Soviet Socialist Republic of Armenia. Both consider Nagorno-Karabakh culturally and religiously significant and worth fighting for. Since most of the population of Nagorno-Karabakh was ethnic Armenian in Stalin's time, this decision laid the seeds for future conflict. When the Soviet Union collapsed in 1991, the future of the region "became central to national movements in Armenia and Azerbaijan. As the two republics gained independence in 1991, the conflict become a fully-fledged war."[4] Turkey was the first country to recognize Azerbaijan's independence after the fall of the Soviet Union and the first to offer support.

The First Nagorno-Karabakh War was a prolonged conflict fought between hastily organized Armenian and Azerbaijani forces using Soviet-era equipment and tactics.

The deep-rooted causes of the war remain an issue of conflict between Baku and Yerevan. Azerbaijan argues that the war was initiated by a land-hungry Armenia eager to seize its territory. Armenia maintains that the war started between Nagorno-Karabakh and Azerbaijan, and that Armenia became engaged only to protect Nagorno-Karabakh's overwhelmingly Armenian population and their right to self-determination. Both sides consider the disputed territory vital to national survival, and a symbol of national aspirations and of the hostility of the other.[5]

The military leaders of both Armenia and Azerbaijan had trained in Soviet military schools, but, during the First Nagorno-Karabakh War, the Armenians were better organized and better led. Finally, after six years of conflict, Armenia defeated Azerbaijan, took possession of Nagorno-Karabakh, and occupied several surrounding regions that belonged to Azerbaijan. The local Azerbaijani population fled or was displaced. Although a ceasefire was negotiated, a peace treaty was never signed. The situation between the two countries became a "frozen conflict" with no resolution. The dislocation of hundreds of thousands of inhabitants only fueled the fire for future conflict.

Casualties on both sides were heavy for these two small countries. Armenia, the victor, suffered nearly 30,000 civilian and military casualties. Azerbaijan, the loser, lost up to 80,000 civilians and military personnel killed or wounded. Hundreds of thousands of civilians were displaced on both sides as Armenians occupied their territorial gains after this hard-fought conflict. "The displaced included about 500,000 Azerbaijanis from areas surrounding Nagorno-Karabakh and the region itself, about 185,000 Azerbaijanis from Armenia, and more than 350,000 Armenians from Azerbaijan."[6] The Armenian population of Nagorno-Karabakh aspired for independence and created the independent Republic of Artsakh, but it was not recognized by anyone, not even Armenia who did not want to sour relations with Russia. Stepanakert became the capital of the republic.

The post-war development of Azerbaijan and Armenia placed both countries on a collision course. The Republic of Artsakh was independent, and declared to be a democracy, but it was totally dependent upon economic, military, cultural, and political support from Armenia. The Azerbaijanis swore revenge and used their wealth generated by the oil fields of Baku to build up their military.

> Armenia is a poor country, dependent on both Russian economic and military assistance and the remittances of the Armenian diaspora. The economic embargo that Turkey and Azerbaijan have imposed on Armenia since the ceasefire in Nagorno-Karabakh further limits the country's opportunities for economic development and trade. By contrast, Azerbaijan possesses rich reserves of gas and oil, whose prices have risen significantly over the last decade, enabling Baku to sharply increase its military spending since 2005–2006. Since 2011, Azerbaijan's defense outlay, at three billion US dollars annually, is as large as the entire Armenian state budget. Between 2010 and 2015, Azerbaijan increased its defense spending from 2.8 to 4.6 per cent of GDP.[7]

The Azerbaijanis used this wealth to create a professional, modern military force. Discarding some of their Soviet-era oriented military doctrine and training, they retrained their officers, non-commissioned officers and soldiers in a hybrid-western methodology, borrowing much from Turkey's military. Turkey is a North Atlantic Treaty Organization (NATO) member, has a very professional military force and is a regional power with regional ambitions.[8]

With Turkey's help, Azerbaijan developed a professional officer corps. Azerbaijani officers were educated in Turkish and Pakistani military schools and developed new tactical methods.

From 2010–2020, Azerbaijan spent US$24–42 billion to prepare its armed forces. The investments were targeted to create asymmetric advantages for Azerbaijan—command and control systems, unmanned precision strike forces, long-range artillery, layered air defense systems (many purchased from Israel and Turkey), and cyber and information war capabilities. In the Russian tradition, the Azerbaijanis stressed long-range artillery fires and tanks, but they also adopted new precision weaponry such as the Israeli-made Harop loitering munition (LM) and the Turkish-made TB2 unmanned combat aerial vehicle. They emphasized the training and leadership of their special forces, expecting these units to bear the brunt of close combat with the Armenians. These advantages gave Azerbaijan a qualitative and technical advantage over the Armenians. Most importantly, the Azerbaijanis relied on Turkey to help them plan and prepare for the pre-emptive war they were waiting to unleash. The Turks were very happy to oblige.[9]

After the First Nagorno-Karabakh War, the Armenians basked in the glories of their past victories and prepared for a repeat of the first war. They spent a valuable portion of their defense budget, and money from donations they received from the large Armenian diaspora, to improve fixed defensive positions, trench lines and bunkers along the Line of Contact with Azerbaijan. These defensive works became known as the Bagramyan and Ohanyan lines. Elaborate trench lines, sited on high ground overlooking the valleys where Azerbaijani attackers would have to ascend, gave the Armenians a solid sense of security. These defenses were particularly strong along the few roads that led through the mountains. The Armenians, and the forces assigned to the Republic of Artsakh, expected any future war would be protracted where they held the high ground in prepared positions, holding the Bagramyan line against the invaders. They also expected the tempo of any future fighting to be like the first war. If the Azerbaijanis attacked, Armenian defenses were strong and there would be plenty of time to mobilize reserves to bolster their unassailable lines.

After Armenia's victory in 1994, Azerbaijan and Turkey demanded Armenia withdraw from Nagorno-Karabakh and seven surrounding districts. Armenia refused and the independent Republic of Artsakh was established. The alliance between Turkey and Azerbaijan became a crucial part of the evolving situation concerning Nagorno-Karabakh. There are significant historical, cultural, linguistic, and economic ties between Turkey and

Azerbaijan, particularly in the military sphere. The militaries of Azerbaijan and Turkey first started working together in 1992 and this bond was strengthened after Azerbaijan's defeat in the First Nagorno-Karabakh War. Turkey helped rebuild, retrain, reorganize and professionalize the Azerbaijani military, gaining from this arrangement through trade and profiting from the importation of oil and natural gas from Azerbaijan's growing energy sector. The pace of Turkish–Azerbaijani military cooperation and training accelerated from 2010–2020. They consider each other as strategic partners and use the slogan "two countries, one nation."

In April 2016, both sides clashed for four days along the Line of Contact (LoC), losing about 500 soldiers each. Azerbaijani special forces attacked across the LoC and captured two villages. Moscow arranged a ceasefire on April 5, but Azerbaijan had demonstrated its forces could fight a modern combat operation. Of note was that the four-day war in 2016 saw the first use by Azerbaijani forces of the Israeli Harop loitering munition.

> For the first time since the 1994-95 ceasefire, Nagorno-Karabakh had to accept the loss of a minor amount of territory to Azerbaijan, despite successfully fending off the Azeri attack. This diminutive territorial gain was celebrated throughout Azerbaijan as a first victory. Armenia, by contrast, experienced a series of disappointments in Russia and the Russia-led Collective Security Treaty Organization (CSTO). Moscow was unwilling to explicitly name the original aggressor, and Russia and the other CSTO states provided Armenia with very little public support, whereas Azerbaijan was fully backed in public by Turkey's President Recep Tayyip Erdoğan.[10]

There were claims from both sides of atrocities committed by the other, including the execution of prisoners and civilians, and the use of banned weapons such as cluster bombs and white phosphorus munitions, but no movement towards a peace settlement was forthcoming.

By 2020, the growing cooperation between the military forces of Azerbaijan and Turkey had transformed the former's military into a more modern and disciplined fighting force. The upgrade was made at the expense of Russia and of those in Azerbaijan who associated with, or were trained by, the Russian military. Russian media reported in 2020 that most of the Russian-trained officers of Azerbaijan's Army were "purged" and that Turkish generals were closely advising Azerbaijan's military.

> According to vz.ru [a Russian military news outlet], the Azerbaijani army is being purged of the officers and generals who started their careers in the Soviet Union and studied in Soviet military schools. Instead, those officers who have completed an internship or a training program in Turkey are placed in key military positions. In addition, Turkish advisers are placed above them.[11]

Armenia, on the other hand, received almost all its training and equipment from Russia. As a member of the Russian-inspired Collective Security Treatment Organization (CSTO), a Russian version of NATO in the Caucasus, Armenia purchased Russian equipment at a discount and its military trained in Russian schools. Russia, however, was playing both sides and traded with Azerbaijan, primarily in military equipment and energy. Although Armenia was totally dependent on Russia for its economy and military, its new government, led by Nikol Pashinyan, hoped to gain more independence from direct Russian control. In early 2020, the President of Russia, Vladimir Putin, reiterated that his country did not recognize Nagorno-Karabakh as part of Armenia and would not consider an attack against the Republic of Artsakh as an attack on a CSTO member state. If the fighting was restricted to Nagorno-Karabakh proper, and did not spill into greater Armenia, the Russians would not interfere. Armenia, therefore, was isolated and on its own if a conflict broke out with Azerbaijan.

During the period July 12–16, 2020, both sides fought again for four days. Armenia restored an abandoned border checkpoint and skirmishing began. Each side engaged the other along the LoC. Azerbaijan claimed they killed 120 Armenians and destroyed one tank, several other armored vehicles and five unmanned aerial vehicles (UAVs). The Armenians reported that they killed 21 Azerbaijani soldiers, and destroyed one tank and 13 UAVs. Each side claimed fewer friendly casualties in their official reports. Azerbaijan also announced the loss of several senior leaders, a Major General Polad Hashimov, a colonel and two majors. Hashimov was a popular general on the rise in the Azerbaijani military and his death to Armenian artillery fire incited widespread anger in Azerbaijan. Infuriated Azerbaijanis called for his death to be avenged and spurred widespread protests across Azerbaijan, particularly in the capital of Baku. Hashimov was the first Azerbaijani general killed in battle.

The most significant point of the July 2020 fighting, however, was the increasingly sophisticated way Azerbaijan used its UAVs. Not only did it use sophisticated Israeli UAVs and LMs to strike, but real-time video from these weapons was used to fight an information war campaign via social media outlets, hoping to demoralize Armenian public support for their government. Armenia should have learned from this, but it appears the fighting was too short to provide impact.

Although the fighting died down by July 30, with occasional exchanges of gunfire and artillery, neither side committed to a lasting ceasefire, let alone a peace settlement. War was in the air with tensions running hot. Prime Minister Nikol Pashinyan of Armenia and President and Commander-in-Chief Ilham Aliyev of Azerbaijan both declared victories. In addition, the

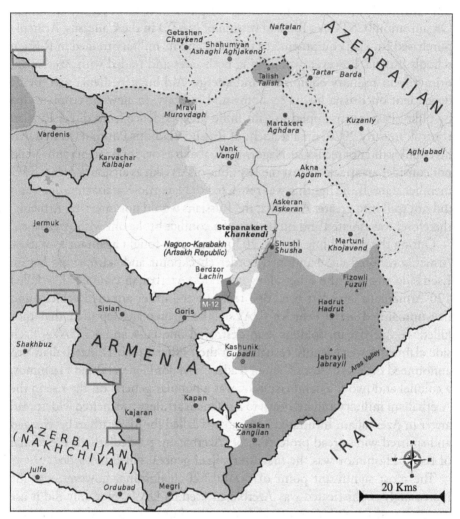

Map 4: 2020 Pre-War Border Clashes. In July 2020, Armenian and Azerbaijani forces clashed in the areas shown above by boxes. The fighting was blamed on Armenia. Sergey Lavrov, Russian Minister of Foreign Affairs, stated that "a trigger of sorts was the geographical factor: Armenia's decision to restore an old border checkpoint, located in 15 kilometers distance [9 miles] from Azerbaijan's export pipelines, caused strong concerns on one side and unwarranted response from the other." Armenia reported it was merely reacting to Azerbaijani forces crossing the border illegally. The July incident resulted in casualties on both sides, including the death of an Azerbaijani general. The July 2020 fighting and the death of the general was considered the spark that ignited the Second Nagorno-Karabakh War on September 27, 2020. (Map Wiki commons)

Armenia's Missile, Multiple Rocket Launch Systems (MRLS) artillery, Unmanned Aerial Systems (UAS), and Loitering Mentions (LM) Arsenal available at the start of the Second Nagorno-Karabakh War

Weapon (by NATO Designations)	Number	Information
SS-26 Stone (Iskander-E (Russian made)	8	Ballistic Missile, 300 km max range
SS-1C Scud B (Russian made)	8	Ballistic Missile, 300 km max range
SS-21 Scarab (9K79 Tochka-U) (Russian made)	4	Ballistic Missile, 120 km max range
BM-30 Smerch (Russian-made MRLS)	6	300mm Rockets, 90 km max range
Norinco WM-80 (Chinese-made MRLS)	4	273mm Rockets 120 km max range
TOS-1A (Russian-made MRLS)		220mm Rockets, 10 km max range
BM-21 Grad (MRLS)		122mm Rockets, 20 km range
Orlan-10 (Russian made)	?	Class 1 UAS
X-55 (Armenian made)	?	Class 1 UAS
Krunk-9 or 11 Crane (Armenian made)	?	Class 1 UAS
HRESH (Armenian-made—PROMAQ)	?	Lass 1 LM, Possibly a copy of the Israeli Hero-30 drone, 20 km range

2020 Covid-19 pandemic affected both but hit Armenia the hardest. In July, Armenia reported 34,001 cases and 620 deaths, while Azerbaijan noted 26,165 Azeris infected and 334 deaths. Leyla Abdullayeva, head of the Press Service Department of Azerbaijan's Foreign Affairs Ministry, reported in an interview with *The Jerusalem Post* that "The situation internally in Armenia is so bad with coronavirus, its leaders want to deviate the attention of the masses." Whether or not this is true, waging war during a pandemic clearly added a new dimension to the conflict and infections spiked in both countries from September to November 2020 during the Second Nagorno-Karabakh War.

Despite the pandemic, Azerbaijan wanted revenge. In the summer of 2020, strong Turkish support bolstered President Aliyev's resolve and gave him confidence. In Armenia, as the developing political and military situation inexorably headed toward a conflict, there was a reluctance to see the gathering storm. Doubtful and hesitant, Armenia seemed to be sleepwalking while Azerbaijan prepared for a war that would retake all the "occupied" lands and restore the country's prestige and power. Armenia, landlocked and isolated without allies, was confident its forces could hold the mountains against any assault. Russia did not want a confrontation with Turkey and searched for ways to avoid triggering the CSTO defense treaty with Armenia. Turkey, the rising regional power in the Caucasus, enabled and encouraged its oil-rich

Azerbaijan's Missile, Multiple Rocket Launch Systems (MRLS) artillery, Unmanned Aerial Systems (UAS), and Loitering Mentions (LM) Arsenal available at the start of the Second Nagorno-Karabakh War

Weapon (by NATO Designations)	Number	Information
LORA Precision Guided Missile (Israeli made)	8	Ballistic Missile, 280 km max range
EXTRA Precision Guided Missile (Israeli made)	6	Ballistic Missile, 150 km max range
SS-21 Scarab (9K79 Tochka-U) (Russian made)	4	Ballistic Missile, 120 km max range
Polonez (Belarusian-made MRLS)	10	300 mm Rockets, 200 km range
TRG-300 Tiger (Turkish-made MRLS)	20	300 mm Rockets, 120km max range
T-300 (Turkish-made MRLS)	20	300 mm Rockets, 120 km max range
BM-30 Smerch (Russian-made MRLS)	30–40	300mm Rockets, 90 km max range
T-122 Sakarya (Turkish-made MRLS)	40	122mm Rockets, 40 km max range
RM-70 (Czech-made MRLS)	30	120 mm Rockets, 20 km max range
T-107 (Turkish-made MRLS)	30	107 mm Rockets, 11 km max range
TOS-1A (Russian-made MRLS)	36	220mm Rockets, 10 km max range
HERMES-900 (Israeli made)	2	Medium Altitude Long Endurance (MALE) Intelligence, surveillance, and reconnaissance (ISR) UAS, 36 hours endurance
HERMES-450 (Israeli made)	10	MALE UAS, 20 hours endurance
HERON	5	MALE UAS, 30 hours endurance
AN-2 COLT (Russian-made biplane)	60	Repurposed as a Remotely Piloted Vehicle (RPV) flying bomb and decoy, max range ~845 km
Bayraktar TB2 (Turkish made)	36	MALE UAS, 24 hours endurance
Aerostar (Israeli made)	14	MALE UAS, 12 hours endurance
Searcher (Israeli made)	5	UAS, 20 hours endurance

Azerbaijani "brothers." Azerbaijan took confidence in the full support and cooperation of Turkey. Both countries held joint military training exercises, involving ground and air operations, in July and August 2020.[12] In September, the Azerbaijanis were ready to execute their plan, codenamed "Operation *Iron Fist*," and began mobilization weeks before the outbreak of hostilities. The Armenians, confident in their mountain defenses, did not mobilize early. Artsrun Hovhannisyan, Press Secretary of the Armenian Ministry of Defense, boasted a few days before the war: "If Azerbaijan starts a war, Armenian tanks will go as far as Baku." By late September, the stage was set.

The guns began firing all along the Line of Contact on September 27, 2020. The war continued for 44 days. (Azerbaijan Ministry of Defense photo).

CHAPTER 2

The Second Nagorno-Karabakh War

"History shows us that no entirely new weapon has radically affected the course of any war; that the decisive weapon in a war has always been known, if but in crude and undeveloped form, in the previous war."

B. H. LIDDELL HART

As the sun rose on Sunday, September 27, 2020, the sky was lit by the fire of rockets and the ground rocked by the explosions of hundreds of artillery shells. Along the Line of Contact (LoC), from the village of Talish in the north, with an Armenian population of about 600, to Martuni Province in the southeast, the Azerbaijani military was on the move against the Armenian forces defending Armenian-controlled Nagorno-Karabakh, what they called the Republic of Artsakh. The defenders where not even in their trench lines when the war started, signifying an intelligence failure that would plague them throughout the coming weeks.

As the guns blasted away along the Nagorno-Karabakh LoC, Armenia and Azerbaijan launched a virtual barrage of invectives in an evolving information campaign. On September 27, the Azerbaijan Foreign Ministry announced: "Another [act of] aggression by Armenia against Azerbaijan is a blatant violation of fundamental norms and principles of international law, international humanitarian law, including the Geneva Conventions of 1949 ..." Armenia's Defense Ministry responded that its troops destroyed three tanks, downed two helicopters and knocked out three unmanned aerial vehicles in response to an attack on civilian targets that included the regional capital of Stepanakert. Azerbaijan replied that its army had launched a "counter-offensive operation along the entire front to suppress the combat activity of the armed forces of Armenia and ensure the safety of the civilian population." Armenia responded that Azerbaijan's attack was a declaration of war, declared martial law, and began mobilizing its reserves. Azerbaijan also declared martial law. Both sides immediately blamed each other for starting the conflict, but it quickly became clear that Azerbaijan had mobilized and prepared prior to the clashes on September 27 and was launching a carefully orchestrated "counter-attack" designed to change the status quo. The next morning, Armenian Defense Ministry spokesperson Shushan Stepanyan reported: "During [the] night, battles continued with different intensity. Early in [the] morning, Azerbaijan resumed its offensive operations, using artillery, armored vehicles, and TOS [Russian-made] heavy artillery system."[1]

The six weeks that followed involved the deliberate implementation of the Azerbaijani plan to take back Nagorno-Karabakh and remove Armenian settlers from what the Azerbaijanis called their "historic lands." Although the Azerbaijani military campaign plan has not yet been released to the public, there have been several open-source articles that outline the plan in multiple phases. From a detailed study of what happened, the war unfolded in three general phases.

Phase 1: Blind, destroy and disrupt key warfighting networks

Armenia was not prepared for what was about to unfold. Confident their defensive lines in the mountains of Nagorno-Karabakh were unassailable, the Armenians developed a passive psyche focused on holding an area defense. As the first day of battle erupted, soldiers from the Artsakh defense force and Armenian Army deployed to their defensive positions as Azerbaijan launched a well-planned offensive. Former Secretary of the Artsakh Security Council (2020), and former Commander of the Defense Army (1993–99), Samvel A. Babayan talked about his experience on the first day of the war and described it as an unmitigated disaster.

> On the morning of September 27, the Armenian side lost 50% of its anti-aircraft forces and 40% of its artillery in 15 minutes. The enemy had satellites looking at us. It happened in 15-20 minutes. If the Armenian side loses 40% of the artillery and 50% of the anti-aircraft, it is a big disaster.

Although Armenia had 26 years since the end of the First Nagorno-Karabakh War to prepare for this day, it was not ready. The elaborate trench lines and bunkers, that may have been well-suited to win the First War, were not camouflaged, prepared or properly defended for the new systems the Armenians would face in the Second War. As events developed, it is doubtful any trench lines without layered and resilient air defense coverage, no matter how well

Map 5: Azerbaijani Battle Plan. This map depicts the general movements of Azerbaijan (AZE) forces during the execution of Operation *Iron Fist*. The numbers represent key terrain features (see Map 3). It also shows the general area of the Armenian defense. As Azerbaijani drones and long-range precision fires shaped the battlespace, Azerbaijan's II Corps conducted the main attack to penetrate the Armenian defenses in the south, capture Hadrut, and then move on to secure the Lachin corridor. Armenian forces blocked the corridor and Azerbaijan continued the attack by infiltrating their special forces to capture Shusha. For a description of the shaded areas of territory, see Map 2. (Map adapted from Wiki Commons)

camouflaged, would have made a difference. "Armenia has an army of the 20th century," reported Sergey Sovetkin, Russian military analyst for *Russian Military Review* on October 2, 2020, "while Azerbaijan has elements of the 21st century. Hence the difference in battle tactics."[2]

The Armenian battle plan appears to have been to rapidly mobilize two self-contained divisions, which operated as small corps, and a separate command for air defense. The Armenians were able to mobilize and deploy about 30,000 troops during the war, but, when they did mobilize, it was only partially effective. The first line unit, the 10th Mountain Rifle Division, positioned in the north and center of Nagorno-Karabakh, consisted of "at least nine motorized rifle regiments, an artillery regiment, a tank brigade, and other divisional subordination units. The second line was the 18th Motorized Rifle Division (in the south), deployed as a second echelon,[3] with at least five mountain rifle regiments. These two divisions were deployed to defend prepared positions on the high ground running north to south. These defenses were referred to as the Bagramyan and Ohanyan lines. The Bagramyan Line consisted of trenches and bunkers established during the First Nagorno-Karabakh War. The Ohanyan Line, named after a former Armenian defense minister, was a trench and bunker defensive zone reinforced with mines and barbed wire that ran across most of the LoC between Armenia and Azerbaijan. Built and upgraded since the First Nagorno-Karabakh War, these fortifications gave the Armenians confidence they could stop any Azerbaijani offensive, even though the bunkers and trenches were designed to stop a 20th century, rather than 21st century, military force. Some of the roads and trails that led through the Ohanyan Line were even blocked by World War II-like steel anti-tank "hedgehogs." That confidence would prove misleading. With a total lack of camouflage or other deceptive techniques, the trench lines were clearly seen from unmanned aerial systems (UASs), loitering munitions (LMs), and aircraft systems flying over the battlespace, and from Azerbaijani and Turkish satellites in low-earth orbit. The Armenians could not hide from Azerbaijan's sensor network.

The Azerbaijanis, on the other hand, were primed and ready. Years before the outbreak of the Second Nagorno-Karabakh War, they were laying the foundation of victory. Valuable lessons were learned from the short four-day war fought against Armenia in 2016. With the close assistance of the Turkish military, the Azerbaijanis planned to outmatch their adversary in the next round of fighting.[4] As A. V. Lavrov, a Russian military analyst said in the 2021 Russian study of the Second Nagorno-Karabakh War, *Storm in the Caucasus*:

The offensive didn't feel like improvisation or a sudden emotional decision of Azerbaijan's leadership: three times in 2020, the armed forces of Azerbaijan and Turkey held joint exercises; twice inspections by the Turkish Armed Forces General Staff checked the combat readiness of the Azerbaijani troops; and on September 22, Azerbaijan seized off-road vehicles from private owners.[5]

In fact, Russian news outlets reported Turkey was involved in both the planning and execution of the war:

> … the group headed by Major General Bahtiyar Ersay, Chief of the Operations Directorate of the Turkish Land Forces of Turkey, directly participated in planning the military campaign against Nagorno-Karabakh … Another Turkish commander who took part in leading the operation in Nagorno-Karabakh is Major General Göksel Kahya, head of the Turkish Air Force's 1st Supply and Maintenance Center … to control the Turkish Bayraktar TB2 drones.[6]

The intent of Operation *Iron Fist* was to capture as much of Nagorno-Karabakh and the "occupied" areas as possible, before the fighting was halted by the major powers, such as Russia, the US or the European Union. Azerbaijani and Turkish planners realized any assaults up steep mountain slopes would result in heavy casualties and would be slow going. To avoid casualties and deliver a more rapid advance, the Azerbaijani plan aimed for precision fires to enable maneuver. Fire without maneuver is indecisive. Maneuver without fire is fatal. The Azerbaijani plan tried to balance both fire and maneuver by leveraging their newly acquired precision strike capability. The concept was to focus on the disintegration of key Armenian networks and systems within a designated strike zone. These networks and systems, in priority, were air defense radars and air defense systems, electronic warfare (EW), command and control, then artillery and rocket forces, tanks, armored vehicles, logistic vehicles and sites, and then troops. The concept was to blind the Armenian defense network, disintegrate the network, then take apart the other systems. To do this the Azerbaijanis were counting primarily on their flying robotic combat systems—unmanned combat aerial vehicles (UCAVs), loitering munitions, and intelligence, surveillance and reconnaissance (ISR) unmanned aerial systems. Whenever possible, artillery and rocket forces would attack Armenian systems identified by the drones. The first step was to deceive and overwhelm the Armenian Soviet-era air defense radars and missile systems, by using decoys and electronic jamming, and then destroy key targets using Turkish and Israeli-made UASs for ISR, and UCAVs and LMs for ISR and strike.

The Azerbaijani ground units consisted of three separate corps and the Azerbaijani special forces (see Map 4). I and III Corps attacked in the center and north, against the most mountainous terrain, while II Corps and the special forces attacked through the Horadiz passage and then along the Aras Valley in the south. I and III Corps' operations intended to pin Armenian forces in place while the main effort of the ground offensive, led by II Corps and the special forces, maneuvered in the south. This southern attack was a larger version of the 2016 assault, this time with full support and ample forces following in echelon and ready to follow through. Most importantly, the special forces were assigned to assist the main effort and take over the fight if the Armenian defenses and restricted terrain stopped II Corps from reaching its objective. The special forces, numbering less than 1,000 soldiers, were trained by Turkey and Pakistan and ranked as one of the best light infantry forces in the Caucasus.

Shortly after Azerbaijani artillery began shelling Armenian positions on September 27, Azerbaijan initiated the assault aimed at the destruction of the opposing air defense network. Every other aspect of the plan depended on this first step. To determine where the main air defense strength of the Armenians was located, Azerbaijan set in motion a sophisticated deception operation. Earlier in 2020, it had purchased 60 1940s-designed, Antonov An-2 biplanes (codenamed "Colt" by the North Atlantic Treaty Organization, NATO). The seller, Russia, was more than happy to sell these ancient aircraft for a good price, not understanding or caring about their intended use. Azerbaijan, most likely with help from the Turks, repurposed these aircraft as unmanned, remotely piloted vehicles (RPVs). They then filled each aircraft with explosives. In the opening phase of the conflict, the Colts were flown against the Armenian air defenses. Flying at a medium altitude so radar would be sure to pick them up, the Armenian air defense network turned on, identified, and then destroyed several of the incoming aircraft.

As the Armenians were congratulating themselves over this victory, the air defense systems that had engaged the incoming RPVs were identified by Azerbaijani ISR UASs and then hit by precision fire attacks from groups of UCAVS and Harop and Orbiter LMs. One report indicated the repurposing of the biplanes was even more rudimentary. "These decoys were quite low-tech: the (Azerbaijani) pilots simply aimed ... the cheap biplanes at Armenian lines, strapped the controls with belts to maintain course, and bailed out. Paired with strike UAS, this proved to be an extremely cost-effective method of revealing and then targeting an enemy air defense."[7] Rapidly, the Azerbaijani precision attack disintegrated the Armenian air defense network. By the second week of the war, the Armenians were reduced to mostly shoulder-fired man portable air defense systems. Azerbaijan won air supremacy in the first few days of the war and now their UASs, UCAVs, and LMs could fly unmolested across the strike zone to hunt Armenian systems.

The term "kill chain" describes the military concept related to the structure of an attack by long-range fires and consists of target identification, force dispatch to target, decision, and order to attack the target, and, finally, the destruction of the target. To optimize the kill chain, Azerbaijani and Turkish planners developed a reconnaissance strike zone, a three dimensional area of space above the battlefield, to engage targets. Since many of the LMs were "human on the loop," where an operator flies the munition to the target area and then orders it to attack, or "human out of the loop" (systems that, once sent into a circling pattern over a target area, would identify and strike a target on its own), the ability to sense and then immediately strike at machine speeds created an accelerated kill chain. A focus of Azerbaijan's expensive investment in its military forces was the purchase of the latest unmanned systems from Israel and Turkey, as well as air defense and ballistic missiles. This provided the Azerbaijan military with an asymmetric precision deep strike capability the Armenians did not possess. The three most important systems in this "reconnaissance-strike" asymmetric capability were the Turkish-made Bayraktar TB2 and the Israeli Harop and Orbiter LMs (see Chapter 3 for more information on each system).

Semi-autonomous Human in the loop	Human-autonomous Human on the loop	Fully autonomous Human out of the loop
Weapon system that, once activated, is intended to only engage individual targets or specific target groups that have been selected by a human operator. Includes "fire and forget" munitions.	An autonomous weapon system that is designed to provide human operators with the ability to intervene and terminate engagements, including in the event of a weapon system failure, before unacceptable levels of damage occur.	A weapon system that, once activated, can select and engage targets without further intervention by a human operator.

Note: Definitions per DoDD 3000.09, Autonomy in Weapon Systems

More important than these "strike" weapons, or "shock drones" as they are often called in Russia, was the depth of sensors Azerbaijan had at its disposal. Ultimately, sensors are more important than strike systems. Without the ability to find targets, the best UCAVs and LMs will merely fly circles in the sky. Turning the battlespace transparent, however, magnifies the potential of precision and non-precision weaponry.

> These sensors multiplied the effectiveness of Azerbaijan's UAs [sic, Unmanned Aerial Systems], ballistic missiles, and older guided missile systems, giving Azerbaijan close-range tactical strike capabilities matched by long-range operational-level strike capabilities. These complementary precision strike capabilities proved to be a game changer tactically, which enabled the Azerbaijanis to overcome well-prepared Armenian defenses on the high ground, and at a higher level of war, an operational game changer that enabled them to isolate the battlespace.[8]

Nearly every day of the war, except for a few days from 7–8 November, when the fog was so thick as to ground many UCAVs and LMs, Azerbaijan had a superior view of the battlespace while the Armenians were relegated to a limited picture generated by only a few unmanned ISR systems.

In the first weeks of the war,

> Bayraktar TB2s frequently operated within range of several 9K33 OSA systems[9] at the same time without ever being targeted. It is likely that Armenia had envisaged that it could at least partially compensate the lack of capabilities of the 9K33 by deploying them in far greater numbers so that their engagement envelopes would overlap. This would mean that if a TB2 was in the process of engaging one 9K33 it would automatically fly into the range of another system located nearby. As Armenia found out the hard way, these systems turned out to be completely unable to identify the Bayraktar TB2s flying circles above them even with their radar system visibly turned on. This was likely the result of the TB2's low radar visibility, and possibly due to the use of electronic warfare (EW) measures by Azerbaijan, resulting in at least 16 9K33 OSA destroyed with no TB2s lost in return.[10]

Turkey possesses a robust synthetic aperture radar (SAR) and ground moving target indicator radar capability. During the war, Turkish drones, aircraft and satellites provided Azerbaijan with enhanced situation awareness and real-time targeting information, covering any gaps in its coverage of the battlespace. Since Turkey is just to the west of Nagorno-Karabakh, Turkish manned and unmanned systems, flying safely in Turkish airspace, could employ their SAR systems to identify and report the location of Armenian forces. These SAR systems are in aircraft that can operate day and night in all weather conditions. A November 7, 2020, *Global Defense Corp* (a military news internet site), report cited that the Turks identified and located Armenian targets and sent the global positioning satellite data to the Azerbaijani drone operators. The report also identified the Turkish E-7A airborne early warning (AEW) aircraft as one of the systems used to coordinate the Azerbaijani battle for air dominance.

> When the E-7A flies at an altitude of 9,000m [29,500 feet], the radar can track 180 targets and has a detection distance of air targets of 600 km [373 miles]. ELINT [Electronic Signals

Intelligence] equipment uses the same antenna and can detect enemy radars up to 850 km [528 miles] ... At the same time, the E-7A AEW is a command and control hub, transmitting and receiving the tactical, air and ground situation to pilots in their planes and to units on the ground ... This way, the Turkish Army General Staff has on the map the location of all Armenian weapons in Nagorno-Karabakh.[11]

If this report is true, the Armenians were fighting a very lopsided fight and their erstwhile ally, Russia, did not come to their aide in any significant manner. The combination of "shock drones" and a sophisticated sensor and battlespace coordination effort by the Azerbaijanis and Turks destroyed the Armenian air defense network and provided Azerbaijan with air dominance for the rest of the war.

By October 4, Azerbaijan announced the capture of the town of Jabrayil in southeast Nagorno-Karabakh. Jabrayil is a "ghost town" abandoned due to the fighting in the First Nagorno-Karabakh War and lies along a critical road that leads northwest toward the town of Hadrut. Azerbaijani President Ilham Aliyev announced in a televised address: "Nagorno-Karabakh is our land. This is the end. We showed them who we are. We are chasing them like dogs." Armenian Prime Minister Pashinyan offered a more conciliatory statement and said his country was ready for "mutual concessions" with Azerbaijan. On October 9, Azerbaijan announced the capture of Hadrut, in the Khojavend District (an area in the west of Nagorno-Karabakh), and eight other villages by the Azerbaijani Army. High-resolution images, from Azerbaijan's Azersky satellites, were published on the internet the day Hadrut was captured. Hadrut was a key victory for Azerbaijan, as the town is the first regional center with an Armenian population in Nagorno-Karabakh. This was also a major blow to Armenian morale. Hadrut was tactically important as military forces can control the approaches to the vital M-12 Highway into Nagorno-Karabakh. The seizure of Hadrut forced Armenian defenders in the Fizuli and Jabrayil regions to withdraw from their prepared positions or risk being cut-off and surrounded. In the next two days, Armenian forces counterattacked, in an attempt to retake Hadrut, but these attacks were poorly coordinated and the Azerbaijanis repulsed every assault.

As this fighting was taking place, a missile war erupted between the two belligerents. Azerbaijan reported it had destroyed missile launch sites in Armenia. Armenia vowed to hit more targets in Azerbaijan. The Israeli-made ballistic missile defenses Azerbaijan purchased were effective in stopping most of the Armenian strikes. Some Armenians may have hoped that, by escalating the missile war, they might trip the conditions for the Russians to come to their aid under the CSTO agreement. Russia announced it would not get involved over Nagorno-Karabakh.

A few weeks before the war between Azerbaijan and Armenia erupted, Russian Defense Minister Sergei Shoigu visited Baku—most likely to discuss Russia's reaction to Azerbaijan's plans to engage in an open conflict in Nagorno-Karabakh. One can safely assume that Russia's position was, as later publicly articulated by the Kremlin in response to Armenia's request for military help under the auspices of the Collective Security Treaty Organization (CSTO), that it would not get involved, because Nagorno-Karabakh is an unrecognized republic, officially being Azeri territory.[12]

Armenia, therefore, was on its own against the Azerbaijani–Turk alliance.

And what about the air forces of Armenia and Azerbaijan? Armenia's air force situation was quite embarrassing. It had just been equipped with new, Russian-made Sukhoi Su-25 (NATO codename "Frogfoot") ground attack aircraft, to complement the existing fleet of Su-30 ("Flanker") fighters, but their readiness rate sat at an abysmal 28 percent.[13] Apparently, missiles for these aircraft were not available during the war, so the Armenian air force stayed largely on the ground. The Azerbaijani Air Force had a total inventory of about 145 aircraft, including Russian-made Su-24 "Fencer" all-weather attack aircraft, Su-25s, MiG-21 "Fishbed," MiG-25 "Foxbat" and MiG-29 "Fulcrum" fighters, and Mi-24 and Mi-35M "Hind" attack helicopters. According to a 2021 study, their aircraft readiness was routinely only 50 percent.[14] The Azerbaijani Air Force flew about 600 sorties during the war, mostly launching stand-off weapons and keeping out of the range of Armenian, and potentially Russian, air defenses. It seems that the Azerbaijanis went to great lengths not to put their pilots in harm's way by using UASs, UCAVs and LMs instead.

Phase 2: Fix Armenian combat power inside the strike zone and shape the battlespace

The next step in the Azerbaijani plan was to find, fix, track and destroy targets within the designated battlespace. During the First Nagorno-Karabakh War, both sides fought each other on the front lines. In this new war, Azerbaijan was able to execute a deep operation with robotic systems to attack Armenian positions everywhere in the designated strike zone. A deep operation has roots in the Soviet theory of "Deep Battle" developed before World War II. The concept involves destroying enemy forces throughout the entire depth of the battlespace. During this phase of the Azerbaijani offensive, unmanned systems in Azerbaijan's arsenal led the fight in the strike zone to destroy Armenian targets. The most logical priority of targets in this effort was: any remaining air defense systems; electronic warfare systems, command and control facilities and headquarters; artillery and rocket forces; tanks; armored vehicles such as BMP infantry fighting vehicles; trucks and wheeled vehicles; and, finally, troops. A deep operation employs multiple attacks, hitting the opponent at many points, destroying key systems that disintegrate his ability to employ combined arms. With the robotic systems at their disposal, the Azerbaijanis were able to induce a catastrophic failure of the enemy's defenses.

With their air defenses destroyed, the Armenians could not defend their EW and artillery systems.

> Almost all [Armenian] towed artillery pieces were placed in pre-prepared pits, which although giving some protection against counter-artillery fire, left them completely exposed to drones hovering overhead. It should thus come as no surprise that no less than 130 artillery pieces were destroyed by Bayraktar TB2 UCAVs alone (out of more than 225 artillery pieces confirmed to have been lost by Armenia in total).[15]

Once the EW and artillery were destroyed, the ability of Armenian infantry and tank units to conduct local counterattacks was severely limited. Once the tanks and BMPs were removed, the infantry could only stand in their trenches and hope to repel an Azerbaijani ground assault. When drone strikes hit trucks and wheeled vehicles hauling supplies and reinforcements, the entire defense weakened. When the drones started hunting troops, Armenian morale began to shatter.

> By the third week of the conflict, these deep strikes were taking a severe toll on the Armenian war effort. Ammunition was beginning to run low at the front, reinforcements were not reaching positions, and the Armenians struggled to mass units in their rear to conduct counterattacks against Azerbaijani breakthroughs. While in the mountainous and forested North the Azerbaijanis continued to make little headway, Azerbaijani forces began to make rapid advances in the South.[16]

Azerbaijan's main effort

The main effort was led by Azerbaijan's II Corps, under the command of Major General Mais Barkhudarov, a "Hero of the 2016 Four-Day War" and a rising star in the Azerbaijani Army. He had the largest share of Azerbaijani combat power, particularly drones, artillery and rocket forces. In addition, the special forces, under the command of Major General Hikmet Mirzayev, another experienced and decorated Azerbaijani officer, supported the main effort.

By destroying the Armenian ability to conduct combined arms counterattacks and fixing the Armenians in their trench lines, the Azerbaijanis gained freedom of maneuver. While Azerbaijani forces attacked along the entire front to pin down the defenders, casualties mounted on both sides. On October 4, the Azerbaijani main effort, led by II Corps, exited the Horadiz passage with minimal casualties and attacked southwest into the Aras Valley. This main effort was led by II Corps, under the command of Major General Mais Barkhudarov. He had the largest share of Azerbaijani combat power, particularly drones, artillery and rocket forces. In addition, the Azerbaijani special forces, under the command of Major General Hikmet Mirzayev, supported the main effort. In previous fighting in 2016, the special forces had performed brilliantly.

> ... [they] demonstrated two essential qualities for this category of troops. The first is a high level of interaction with other branches of the military, especially with the artillery battalions; they demonstrated a good level of adjustment of the artillery and MLRS [multiple launch rocket systems], including on related subjects located behind the enemy lines (the use of drones to correct the location is not always the best option). Secondly, the ability to perform tasks independently, in the depths of the enemy's defense (20 km).[17]

By October 17, the battle was tipping in Azerbaijan's favor. Doctor Can Kasapoglu, the director of the Security and Defense Research Program at the Istanbul-based think-tank EDAM (Ekonomi ve Dış Politika Araştırmalar Merkezi, The Centre for Economics and Foreign Policy Studies), reported that the Armenian forces were quickly routed in an "irregular and undisciplined withdrawal" from the frontline positions they'd been fortifying along the 'line of contact' since a 1994 cease-fire brought an end to the previous war."[18] Eric Chan, writing for *The Diplomat* online newsletter put it succinctly:

> For the Armenians, this proved to be fatal. While there was some understanding prior to the outbreak of war that a static "trench defense" was precisely what the Azerbaijanis were prepared to fight against, the slow rate of change meant that Armenia ended up with a flood of volunteers trained by veterans of the 1994 war with wooden guns to execute trench defense. These forces were then correspondingly demoralized by a way of war that had nothing to do with the old Soviet firepower-attrition method that gave Armenia the victory in 1994. The Armenians were fixed and then destroyed – not just in position, but mentally as well.[19]

The famous American World War II general George S. Patton, Jr. said, "Untutored courage is useless in the face of educated bullets." In the Second Nagorno-Karabakh War, the Turkish drones and Azerbaijani LMs were brilliant. The Armenians, no matter how brave, could not stand against such a precision onslaught.

In an effort to add an information war victory to advances on the ground, on October 17, Azerbaijani President Aliyev announced:

… the list of the destroyed Armenian equipment includes: 234 tanks have been destroyed, 36 tanks have been taken as military booty, 49 infantry fighting vehicles have been destroyed, 24 have been taken as military booty, 16 self-propelled artillery pieces have been destroyed, 190 cannons of various calibers, two "Hurricane" systems, one TOS flame-thrower, two "Elbrus" operational tactical missile complexes, one "TOCHKA-U," 35 "OSA" anti-aircraft missile systems, three "TOR" anti-aircraft missile complexes, five "KUB" and "KRUG" anti-aircraft missile complexes, nine radio-electronic combat systems, two S-300 anti-aircraft missile systems, 196 trucks have been destroyed, and 98 have been taken as booty.[20]

Armenia disputes these numbers, but the drone footage Azerbaijan and Turkey saturated the internet and social media with had a telling effect on their enemy's morale. Armenia had not invested in the same class of sensor and strike drones as Azerbaijan. As a result, the high-definition videos produced by these drones, and used by Azerbaijani and Turkish information warfare teams, had a dramatic effect on the Armenian home front. Mothers closely scanned dozens of strike videos on social media, hoping their sons were not in one. Never before in the history of warfare has an information war campaign had such immediate and dramatic high-quality video footage. By October 20, the Aras Valley, and the stretch of land bordering Nagorno-Karabakh and Iran, was completely under Azerbaijani control.

At the same time as the fighting was occurring, the information war was being waged on Twitter, Facebook, and YouTube. Winning the information war was a part of Azerbaijan's shaping operations and the Armenians fought back in kind. As of September 2020, the US Department of Defense did not have an established definition for information warfare. A good definition was provided by Commander Mike Dahm, US Navy (Retired) as "offensive and defensive actions in physical and virtual space that enable and protect the friendly force's ability to access, process, and communicate information that also deny, exploit, corrupt or destroy an adversary force's ability to use information."[21] Even this definition does not go far enough to express how an information war can impact the opponent's morale by waging a messaging campaign on the internet and social media outlets. The high-definition drone videos mentioned before are one example. Azerbaijan often used these videos to exaggerate their effects and the decapitation of Armenian leaders. "During the 44-day war, the Azerbaijani media published many false reports about the deaths of Armenian soldiers, generals, and members of the political leadership. Also, journalists and officials made statements about large-scale losses on the Armenian side."[22]

An example of information war messaging during the shaping phase of the Azerbaijani offensive is a report by *TRT World*, a Turkish media enterprise and strongly pro-Azerbaijani, on October 23. In this report, most of the talking points of the government or Azerbaijan were expressed, especially push back on a story about foreign mercenaries. *TRT* interviewed Fariz Ismailzade, the Vice Rector for External, Government and Student Affairs at the ADA University in Baku, Azerbaijan:

> [The]Azerbaijani army is very professional, organized and motivated. They fight without any foreign help and they are eager to liberate the occupied territories. The Armenian defense line turned out to be very weak and [the] Azerbaijani army broke it very fast. Armenian myth is gone ... It is clear that [the] Azerbaijani side is using Turkish drones and Israeli technology, and this gives them clear superiority. [The] Armenian army has no drones and lost many tanks and other military equipment which [Azerbaijan] ... estimated at $4.6 billion. All Armenia does so far is to launch SCUD missiles to Ganja and other towns of Azerbaijan far from the conflict area and killing kids there.[23]

From reports like this one, and the constant barrage on social media of full-motion videos of successful drone strikes, Azerbaijan won the information war and shaped the battlespace for the next phase of Operation *Iron Fist*.

Phase 3: Maneuver to capture the center of gravity by seizing the decisive terrain

By October 23, Azerbaijan was ready for the final push to gain as much as possible before Russia either intervened or forced a ceasefire. The Turkish and Azerbaijani general staff knew time was not on their side. In October, at least three ceasefires brokered by Russia, France, and the United States were attempted but quickly broken. After the second week of fighting, Armenia was pressing Russia to arrange any ceasefire possible to freeze the Azeri advance. Azerbaijan and Turkey, on the other hand, were unwilling to stop the attack with the tide of battle going in their favor.

Armenian losses were horrific and the destruction of so much equipment and material presented the Armenian and Artsakh leadership with few options. Their way of war, rooted in the combined arms concepts of the last war, and fixated to defending prepared positions, was failing fast against the Azerbaijani high-tech assault. "The first lesson that the Azerbaijani–Armenian clashes showed is the vulnerability of traditional land units—armored, mechanized, and motorized formations—in the face of advanced drone warfare weaponry and concepts," wrote Dr. Can Kasapoglu, the director of the Security and Defense Research Program at the Istanbul-based think-tank EDAM in an article dated October 30, 2020. "At the time of writing, open source intelligence publications documented some 175 main battle losses for the

Armenian occupation forces in Nagorno Karabakh [sic]."[24] Those losses were catalogued shortly after each strike by the *Oryx* blog operated by Belgium military analysts Stijn Mitzer and Joost Oliemans.[25]

The Armenians hunkered down in their trench lines, pressed day and night by drone attacks across the width and depth of the Nagorno-Karabakh battlespace. Armenian troops were shackled by the persistent fear, real or imagined, of an attack from above that could come at any time and any place. Against the drone onslaught, the Armenians had no place to hide and nowhere to run. In this phase of the war, they appeared to be stunned and unable to respond. As their air defense, artillery and counterattack capabilities were negligible, their options seemed bleak. Reports of Armenian units disobeying orders or deserting were reported. The words of Carl von Clausewitz had warned that defenders in mountainous terrain should "Never depend completely on the strength of the terrain and consequently never be enticed into passive defense by a strong terrain." At this point, the Armenians had only the passive defense of their mountain positions left. As the Azerbaijanis moved closer to the M-12 Highway, the Armenians hoped to stop them in the narrow passes.

Comparison to the Yom Kippur War of 1973

In the first week of the Yom Kippur War, the Israelis adapted, improvised and overcame disruption. They did this by rapidly assessing the changes; rapidly adapting their tactics, techniques and procedures; and by taking bold operational and tactical decisions. In the Second Nagorno-Karabakh War, the Armenians did not. Their command and forces were paralyzed. Their reactions were a matter of too little, too late. Once tipped, the Armenians never regained their balance.

There is an interesting parallel to make at this point in the Second Nagorno-Karabakh War. In nearly every conflict, there is a decisive point where the defender either rallies or falls apart. In 1973, the Israel Defense Forces (IDF) faced a similar situation. The methods of war were changing and the IDF had not recognized the changes in time. The surprise attack by the Egyptians and Syrians in 1973 had disproven many of the IDF's basic assumptions about the methods of waging war. "We thought our tanks could stop the Egyptians from putting up bridges but we didn't imagine the forest of antitank missiles," Moshe Dayan, Israel's Minister of Defense in 1973, was quoted as saying during the initial days of the Yom Kippur War. "The air force had plans for eliminating the antiaircraft missiles but they didn't work. We have to learn life anew." In the first week of the Yom Kippur War, the Israelis adapted, improvised and overcame this disruption. They did this by rapidly assessing the changes; rapidly adapting their tactics, techniques and procedures; and taking bold operational and tactical decisions. In the Second Nagorno-Karabakh War, the Armenians did not. Their command and forces were paralyzed. Their reactions were a matter of too little, too late. Once tipped, the Armenians never regained their balance.

With the Armenians unable to maneuver as precision attacks by drones kept them mostly pinned to their defensive lines, the Azerbaijanis moved to secure key villages and open approaches to the Lachin corridor and the M-12 Highway. Gaining control of the highway, or at least holding a portion of it and thus blocking Armenian movement, would be a vital step to winning the war. The focus of Azerbaijan's military command now shifted to the prize: seizure of the mountain plateau city of Shusha. In the case of Shusha, the city was not only located on decisive terrain (decisive terrain is key terrain whose seizure and retention is mandatory for successful mission accomplishment) but its seizure was, understandably, also the decisive point of the war.[26]

Shusha

The hilltop city of Shusha is considered a fortress by both the Azerbaijanis and the Armenians and is a defender's dream. It not only dominates the Lachin road, but there are only three access roads into the city, two in the south and one in the north.

The city of Shusha is a cultural treasure to both the Armenians and Azerbaijanis. Both sides pledged to fight fiercely for Shusha. The hilltop city sits on a high plateau that commands the approaches to the M-12 Highway, the single road that connects Lachin in the southwest and Stepanakert to the north. The city itself is considered a fortress by both the Azerbaijanis and the Armenians and is a defender's dream. It not only dominates the Lachin road, but there are only three access roads into the city, two in the south and one in the north. Once Azerbaijan's II Corps was on the M-12 Highway and within striking distance of Shusha, they attempted a quick rush to overwhelm the defenses. Sensing success, tanks, mechanized infantry and SandCat weapons carriers[27]

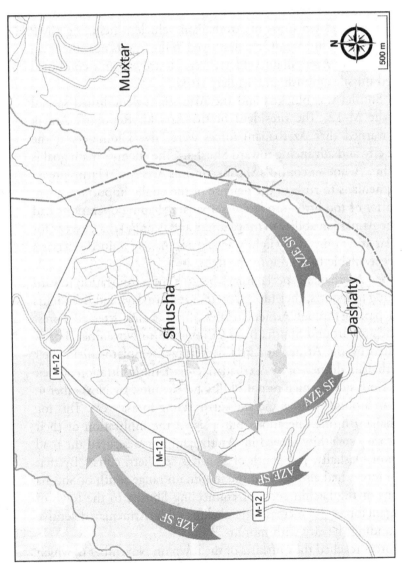

Map 6: Infiltration Attack on Shusha. This map depicts the probable infiltration routes of Azerbaijani special forces into the city of Shusha. It is reported in other open sources that the special forces approached the city from multiple directions and that some even scaled steep cliffs to get past the defenders. Since there is no open-source report to provide the definitive Azeri infiltration plan, this image is provided to illustrate the difficult task Azerbaijani special forces performed to capture the city. Note: The road at the bottom left of this photo is the M-12 Highway. (Map modified by the author from Google Maps)

were sent forward along the narrow road to Shusha. The Armenians were waiting and here, for nearly the first time in the war, they could accurately declare they were able to repulse the Azerbaijani attack. Armenian videos of "Hell's Gorge" showed destroyed Azerbaijani BMPs and dead soldiers lying along the road. A video released by Armenian Zinuzh Media displayed the wrecked hulks of at least ten units of Azerbaijani vehicles, including BMP infantry fighting vehicles and SandCats, destroyed in the forests near the town of Lachin. Most of the Azerbaijani vehicles were destroyed in a combined anti-tank guided missile ambush and artillery strike.

The road to Shusha was blocked and the Armenians demolished several bridges along the M-12. The president of the Artsakh Republic, Arayik Harutyunyan, warned that Azerbaijani forces were "five kilometers at the most" from the city and advancing toward Shusha. "The enemy's main goal is to capture Shushi ... whoever controls Shushi controls Artsakh." Harutyunyan called on all Armenians to rush to the defense of the vitally important town, but it was a matter of too little, too late. Azerbaijani shaping operations had so decimated the Armenian ability to move forces and supplies that, except for a very few regular army units, only lightly armed and poorly trained reservists and militia were available to send into the fight.

On 25 October, Azerbaijani special forces began a mass infiltration toward Shusha. According to reports, they moved on foot for five days and five nights to reach Shusha, passing through Armenian lines without being detected. Forest fires raged in the area around Shusha from October 28 to November 3 or 4, possibly instigated by the Armenians in a desperate attempt to shield their forces from Azerbaijani drones, or by Azerbaijan to mask the infiltration of their special forces.[28] Both sides denied responsibility for the fires. By November 4, a heavy fog set in around Shusha and the surrounding forest areas. This fog inhibited Azerbaijani drone operations but assisted the infiltration of their special forces as they stealthily moved in. Azerbaijani forces secured the road near the village of Dashalty, just south of Shusha's southern cliffs. "By that day, Azerbaijani forces had also secured the mountain range south of Shusha and key portions of the Lachin corridor connecting Shusha to the town of Lachin. Azerbaijani forces also increased the shelling of the Armenian defensive positions surrounding the city with mortars."[29]

The special forces reached the outskirts of the town on November 6, which was another day of thick fog. They then approached Shusha from multiple directions, in groups of about 100 men, attempting to avoid contact until they moved into their designated objectives inside the city. It was a slow and stealthy process, and they had to carry personal weapons, guided anti-tank missiles, food, water and equipment to sustain them in their mission. Samir Bakhshaliyev, who was assigned to the special forces for the infiltration attack on Shusha, said in an interview that one detachment blocked the M-12 Highway to stop any reinforcement of Shusha from the southwest.[30] A team secured the hamlet of Dashalty while another group moved around the city from the eastern side. The eastern side comprised steep cliffs, some 30 meters (100 feet) high. Samir reported they did not think the Armenians were defending the cliffs as they seemed an unlikely and nearly impossible avenue of approach. Counting on this, and under the cover of night and fog, the soldiers climbed the cliffs and infiltrated the city without being discovered.

Once in the city, the individual groups occupied defensive positions. "They established additional blocking positions and ambush sites around the city to further prevent the defending Armenians from being reinforced or resupplied."[31] One group occupied the castle. When the fighting began, most likely in daylight, the Armenians found Azerbaijanis firing from key points in the city. At this point the Armenians were demoralized and running low on everything. When Armenian commanders asked for artillery support, they were told there was none to provide.

> With 20–30 salvos of Smerch we can destroy all Azeri forces in Shusha. We take the town back. But then what? The condition of the army does not allow us to continue the war. Yesterday, I tried to organize an operation with three battalions. We have only four howitzers. Without the artillery, how can we advance? Imagine, for the entire army we only have two Grads, and about 10 howitzers for which we have no rounds.[32]

The Armenians used the fog as cover to launch tanks and BMP infantry fighting vehicles against the invaders, but the advancing armor was either destroyed or forced back by anti-tank weapons. The Armenians launched at least three counterattacks but made no headway towards dislodging the Azerbaijanis. The fighting went on with heavy casualties on both sides. Sometime on November 6, the senior Armenian leaders, including Argishti Kyaramyan, who had been appointed the commander of the Armenian forces in Shusha, abandoned the city.

The heavy fog began to lift the next day and the Azerbaijani TB2 UCAVs and LMs could once again operate against Armenian targets. By the afternoon of 7 November, Shusha was mostly in Azerbaijani hands.

> On the morning of November 8, the Artsakh Ministry of Defense reported that intensive fighting had taken place through the entire night along the length of the front line surrounding Shusha. Armenia also claimed that its forces had downed three Azerbaijani TB2 Bayraktar unmanned aerial vehicles and had destroyed twenty armored vehicles and four tanks throughout the day.[33]

These false reports were denied by Azerbaijan and did not match with the situation on the ground. Without leadership, the Armenian forces fled Shusha for Stepanakert and paid dearly in the process under the enemy's guns. The Armenian leadership knew they had lost the fight for Shusha[34] and sued for peace. As the sun rose on November 8, the Azerbaijanis had won the city.

The Battle of Shusha was the decisive point of the Second Nagorno-Karabakh War. In the end, the decisive terrain and the key objective of the war was captured by light infantry special forces teams using small arms, shoulder-fired anti-tank missiles, and bayonets. The skill, superior training, and leadership of the Azerbaijani special forces gained the upper hand over the confused and demoralized Armenian defenders.

> Despite all the coverage, the lessons missed about the Nagorno-Karabakh War are the ones showing how urban warfare remains a key part of modern combat. The most important battle of the Nagorno-Karabakh War occurred in the city of Shusha. Once Shusha fell, Armenia surrendered and entered a lopsided agreement, ceding massive amounts of their previously held territories.[35]

Azerbaijan's president proudly announced:

> We have destroyed the enemy in an almost hand-to-hand battle, crossing ravines, forests and mountains with light weapons, and liberated Shusha, the crown of Karabakh … We were strengthening the combat capability of our army because it was clear that victory could not be won by weapons alone. It is a soldier and an officer who raises the flag, raises the flag on the enemy's positions, raises it on liberated lands. Our soldiers and officers fought like lions.[36]

Late on November 9, Armenia, Azerbaijan and Russia signed an agreement to end the conflict and bring Russian peacekeepers into the region. Russia brokered a ceasefire that both sides accepted. Armenia's President Pashinyan was desperate for a ceasefire and feared the fall of Stepanakert to Azerbaijan forces. Azerbaijani President Aliyev understood his forces were at the end of their logistics line, had fought a hard battle to win Shusha, and needed to consolidate their gains. They had risked much, taken about as many casualties as they had inflicted on Armenia, and won a tremendous victory beyond their expectations. Armenia had acceded to all their demands for territory, virtually surrendering. The Azerbaijani victory was dramatic and decisive. Armenia's defeat was humiliating and catastrophic. The war ended in this ceasefire, but without a peace treaty. On November 13, following the ceasefire agreement, Russian peacekeepers deployed to the outskirts of Shusha. As they traveled up the road from Stepanakert to Shusha, a *Reuters* reporter took the photos of piles of dead Armenian soldiers, militia, and destroyed vehicles lining the

Map 7: Ceasefire agreement of November 9, 2020. Under the agreement, the warring sides kept control of the areas they held within Nagorno-Karabakh at the time of the ceasefire, while Armenia returned the surrounding territories it occupied in 1994 to Azerbaijan. Azerbaijan also gained transport communication to its Nakhchivan ("Naxcivan" on this map) exclave bordering Turkey and Iran. (Map courtesy of *Radio Free Europe/Radio Liberty*)

road. For Azerbaijan, the slaughter had come in the pursuit, and they had chased the fleeing Armenians nearly to the gates of Stepanakert.

On November 10, Armenia's Minister of Defense Davit Tonoyan said the "... situation in Artsakh is now calm and all military operations have stopped. Russian peacekeepers are quickly coming into the region; they are entering from Armenia through Goris, Lachin, toward Stepanakert." Tonoyan added that "Armenian forces ... had serious problems with the capacity of Azerbaijan's air power and although Armenia's air defense units were able to occasionally shoot down drones, etc., in this kind of fifth generation war, Armenian forces were no longer able to resist."[37]

According to the Center for Eastern Studies, a think-tank in Warsaw, Poland, "The ceasefire at the present stage of the fighting, and in the form outlined above, means a triumph for Azerbaijan and the de facto capitulation of Armenia, which is losing most of the territory it occupied in the early 1990s."[38] The Russian 15th Mechanized Brigade was dispatched to perform peacekeeping operations and deployed along a demarcation line. Russian forces were also placed not far from Shusha, negating any further moves by Azerbaijani forces toward Stepanakert.

> Operating in a region regarded by Russia as its "near abroad," Turkey had given unprecedented support to Azerbaijan, directing the Azerbaijani offensive and bolstering it with combat drones ... a clear threat to Moscow's sphere of influence. Despite the moniker of peacekeepers, analysts regard the Russian troops as simply a tool to push back against Turkey's postwar presence, with the added benefits of opening up trade routes and linking the administration of Armenian Prime Minister Nikol Pashinyan to the Kremlin.[39]

The ceasefire ended the Second Nagorno-Karabakh War and the guns fell silent. Azerbaijan was triumphant and celebrated by holding an elaborate victory parade in Baku on December 10. As the troops marched past the reviewing stand, President Aliyev stood side-by-side with Turkish President Erdoğan. Both leaders had much to celebrate. Aliyev had secured his powerbase through a victorious war. He decorated Selçuk Bayraktar, the developer of the TB2 UCAV system and Erdoğan's son-in-law, for the decisive contribution the TB2s played in winning the war. For Turkey, the war was another step in its rise as a regional power. Erdoğan had extended Turkish military might, economic interests and influence. He had successfully dealt with Russia and the world powers. The successful war also reinforced the alliance between Turkey and Azerbaijan. The Turks celebrated the victory as much as Azerbaijan.

Armenia, on the other hand, experienced a catastrophe. The raw truth was exposed for all to see. The myth of Armenian invincibility, that had grown from the victory in the First Nagorno-Karabakh War, was shattered. The entire nation and diaspora were devastated and humiliated by the defeat. The loss of most of Nagorno-Karabakh forced Armenia into an uncertain future. Armenian political, economic and social life sunk into a vortex. Russia had not come to their aid during the war, as many Armenians had hoped, and the result of the disaster left the country weakened, wounded, and without hope. For many, the only salvation possible was to "embrace the bear" and align more closely with Russia. This is the fate of nations decisively defeated in war. The Armenians learned, as Ernest Hemingway once stated, "defeat brings worse things than any that can ever happen in war."

"The most powerful aircraft of the future will be unmanned aerial vehicles," Baykar's Technical Director Selçuk Bayraktar predicted in an interview with *CNN Türk* on September 16, 2021. Bayraktar is the Massachusetts Institute of Technology educated entrepreneur behind Turkey's thriving combat drone industry. The Bayraktar TB2, shown above, was a key weapon in the 44-day Azerbaijani victory over Armenia in the Second Nagorno-Karabakh War. The TB2 merges "find" capabilities with "strike." The most powerful trend exemplified by the Second Nagorno-Karabakh War is for Intelligence Surveillance and Reconnaissance (ISR) systems to merge ISR and strike capabilities into the same platform. Future systems will be smaller, lighter, unmanned, and armed with long-range precision-guided munitions. (Turkish Defense Industries SSB photo)

CHAPTER 3

When Sensors are Shooters

"Right now, we have some success doing that in less than 20 seconds."
GENERAL MIKE MURRAY, COMMANDER, US ARMY FUTURES COMMAND,
SEPTEMBER 2020, WHEN EXPLAINING TO REPORTERS THE LATEST CAPABILITY TO TIE
SENSORS TO SHOOTERS, FROM START TO FINISH, SENSOR TO SHOTS FIRED.

The Second Nagorno-Karabakh War provided a vivid impression of wars to come. In the past, intelligence, surveillance, and reconnaissance (ISR) platforms primarily found targets for other systems to destroy. The recent fighting in the Caucasus, which involved two near-equal medium powers, has shown how ISR and precision-guided munitions (PGMs) are now blending to become one. During this conflict, the Azerbaijani forces used strike systems, unmanned combat aerial vehicles (UCAVs) and loitering munitions (LMs) to provide critical ISR information. These systems had high-end, active sensors that generated real-time intelligence during combat. In addition, they provided accurate, real-time, battle damage assessment. In the next few years, strike systems will become smaller, faster, less expensive, and better networked. Multipurpose systems that merge sensor platforms with precision-guided strike munitions can dramatically shorten the kill chain. The lessons learned for next-generation ISR from this conflict were dramatic and were key factors in Azerbaijan's decisive victory. Some of the primary systems used by Azerbaijan, principally the TB2 UCAV[1] and the Harop LM,[2] provide an important insight into the future of ISR/Strike systems.

The TB2 UCAV

The Bayraktar TB2 medium-altitude, long-endurance UCAV was the star of the Azerbaijani war effort and is the premier product of the family-run Turkish defense company Baykar. Headquartered in Istanbul, Baykar operates under

Turkey's TB2 UCAV, with its distinctive triangular tail section and loaded with "Roketsan MAM-L and MAM-C micro-missiles," was a major factor in Azerbaijan's war with Armenia in late 2020. According to Baykar Defense, the "TB2 is a Tactical Armed / UAV [unmanned aerial vehicle] System, developed and manufactured by Baykar and a highly sophisticated design that provides all solutions that operators may need in one integrated system. The system consists of Bayraktar TB2 Armed / UAV Platform, Ground Control Station, Ground Data Terminal, Remote Display Terminal, Advanced Base with Generator and Trailer modules ... [the TB2's] Baykar Real Time Imagery Transmission System (BGAM) provides real-time image transmission and processing solutions ... [that] allows high-resolution, non-delay live broadcasts to be monitored by multiple users at the same time. BGAM is a web-based application that allows users to watch live broadcasts securely on the network or on tablets using the mobile application via internet. The system automatically stores all transmitted imagery into 30-minute files. While monitoring live imagery, users can take multi-tag notes on the system. Saved tags and labels will facilitate, at a later date, the search through archive videos. In a similar way, based on these notes, a mission log can be created and then exported. Archived files can be filtered by date and by metadata." During the Second Nagorno-Karabakh War, the video feeds from the TB2 were instrumental in Azerbaijan's efforts to win the information war. (Bayhaluk photo)

the names "Baykar Savunma" (Baykar Defense) and "Baykar Makina Sanayi ve Ticaret A.Ş." (Baykar Machine Industry and Trade Inc.). The Chief Technical Officer of Baykar Makina, Selçuk Bayraktar, studied UAV development while earning his master's degrees at the University of Pennsylvania, and later the Massachusetts Institute of Technology. He is also the son-in-law of Turkish President Recep Tayyip Erdoğan.

The TB2 is Turkey's first indigenous armed-reconnaissance UCAV. Operators on the ground pilot the unmanned craft from a ground control station (GCS) by direct radio link or, in the case of the new satellite receiver equipped TB2S,[3] via Turkey's TüRKSAT satellite network. During the Second Nagorno-Karabakh War, the TB2 found and destroyed Armenian tanks, infantry fighting vehicles, artillery, and infantry positions. The impressive confirmed-kill list of targets included the BM-30 Smerch (the Russian

"Tornado" or "Whirlwind") Multiple Launch Rocket System (MLRS), the 9K3cket3 OSA (what NATO calls the SA-8 "Gecko"), and five S-300 (NATO's SA-10 "Grumble") air defense systems. Of the 200 artillery pieces confirmed lost by Armenia, they claimed the TB2s destroyed 120.

The TB2 is 6.5 meters (21.3 feet) long, with a wingspan of 12 meters (39.4 feet), a distinctive inverted V-tail, and a pusher propeller. The two-blade, variable pitch propeller is powered by a 75-kilowatt (100-horsepower) Rotax 912 gasoline internal combustion engine. The TB2's cruising speed is 70 knots, and the maximum speed is 135 knots. Cruising altitude is 22,500 feet with a maximum of 25,000 feet. Although a Turkish design, many of the original components, including the transponder, engine, electro-optical (EO), micro-munition bomb rack, and other technologies, come from other countries, many of them members of NATO. Some of these manufacturers stopped selling their products directly to Turkey when Armenian social media displayed manufacturer logos and component markings from the wreckage of several TB2s downed in the fighting. Turkey is now working with Ukraine and other suppliers to secure an alternative source for engines, EO systems and miscellaneous components.

To engage targets identified by its EO sensors, the UCAV carries Turkish MAM (Mini Akıllı Mühimmat, Smart Micro Munition) laser-guided smart micro-munitions developed by Turkish defense manufacturer Roketsan. The TB2 has four hard-points that can carry two MAM-C and two MAM-L micro-munitions, or four MAM-Ls. The MAM-C has a multipurpose warhead (blast fragmentation, incendiary and armor piercing); there is also a high-explosive blast fragmentation variant. The MAM-C weighs 6.5 kilograms (14lb), is 70mm (2.75 inches) long, and has a range of 8 kilometers (5 miles). The MAM-L has a tandem warhead variant, effective against reactive armor, and high-explosive blast fragmentation, and thermobaric, versions.[4] The MAM-L weighs only 22 kilograms (48.5lb), and is one meter (3.3 feet) long, and can be used to engage stationary or moving targets with high precision within a range of 8 kilometers (5 miles). The range can be extended to 14 kilometers (8.5 miles) with the inertial navigation system/global positioning system option. Selçuk Yaşar, president and CEO of Roketsan, emphasized the multi-role ISR and strike capability of the TB2:

The design and application concept of the Smart Micro Guided Munitions allow operators to effectively neutralize time-critical targets, particularly those that arise during reconnaissance and surveillance missions. Meanwhile, thanks to their precision guidance and small dimensions, they offer a solution with a low collateral damage. When compared with all the other capabilities of the armed forces, a combination of the Smart Micro Guided Munitions and a tactical UAV is the most cost-effective solution. We believe that other countries will also start taking an interest in this solution soon.[5]

With the success the TB2 experienced during the Second Nagorno-Karabakh War, Roketsan is exporting the system to new customers around the world, including Ukraine and Pakistan. According to *Jane's World Air Forces 2020*, Azerbaijan had at least 36 TB2s during the Second Nagorno-Karabakh War.

The Harop

The Harop is a "kamikaze drone," a loitering attack weapon that combines the characteristics of a missile and a UAV and is designed to locate and precisely engage stationary or moving targets. The LM concept is not new, but Israel Aerospace Industries (IAI) has turned the idea into a war-winning solution, particularly for military forces that do not have access to other long-range, precision-guided options. IAI designed and produced the Harop LM in the early 2000s. Turkey became one of IAI's first customers for Harop in 2005 and successfully employed the system in combat in Libya in 2018–2020. Turkey's ally, Azerbaijan, then became a major customer and IAI sold the system in ample quantities to the Azerbaijani military several years before the Second Nagorno-Karabakh War. The Harop's primary purpose is to attack radar and anti-aircraft systems but, during the war, it destroyed a wide range of targets that included air defense systems, command posts, and convoys of Armenian soldiers traveling to the front lines. The shrill scream the Harop generates during its terminal dive is reminiscent of the World War II-era German Stuka dive-bomber and had an equally demoralizing effect. When Armenian soldiers spotted or heard the Harop, they knew they had seven seconds to take cover before it struck. One Armenian soldier stated: "There was no place to hide and no way to fight back."

The Harop is EO-guided and provides high-definition video of its flight and terminal attack. Accuracy is within 1–2 meters. The Harop is 2.5 meters (8.2 feet) long, with a wingspan of 3 meters (10 feet), and weighs approximately 135 kilograms (300lb), including a 23-kilogram (50lb) high-explosive (HE) fragmentation warhead. It has a nine-hour flight endurance, a range of about 1,000 kilometers (621 miles), and a maximum speed of about 225 knots. During a mission, the Harop can loiter, identify prescribed targets, and dive into a target, or, if no appropriate targets are identified, autonomously return to a designated landing strip. With its impressive range and loitering time of approximately six hours, the system can fly autonomously to a designated

According to Israel Aerospace Industries, "the HAROP Loitering Munition (LM) is programmed before launch by the Ground Control Station (GCS) to autonomously fly to a pre-defined "Holding Area," where they loiter. The Mission Control Station (MCS), in communications with the HAROP, periodically checks their position and status during the route to the "Holding Area." The MCS operator can thus control several HAROP LMs that loiter over a "Holding Area," and can select one LM for target search and attack, while the others are monitored periodically. The operator directs the selected LM to the target area and uses the video image to select a target, and to attack it. The HAROP tracks the target and then dives on it, detonating the warhead upon impact. If required, the attack can be aborted and the operator can re-attack with the same LM." (IAI photo)

strike zone to identify targets that meet its targeting parameters. A human operator then gives the weapon the order to attack. According to IAI:

> The HAROP LMs are programmed before launch by the Ground Control Station (GCS) to autonomously fly to a pre-defined "Holding Area," where they loiter. The MCS (mission control system) periodically checks their position and status during the route to the "Holding Area." The MCS operator can thus control a number of HAROP LMs that loiter over a "Holding Area," select one LM for target search and attack, while the others are monitored periodically. The operator directs the selected LM to the target area and uses the video image to select a target, and to attack it. The HAROP tracks the target and then dives on it, detonating the warhead upon impact. If required, the attack can be aborted, and the operator can re-attack with the same LM.[6]

Harops can be fired from truck-mounted "MLRS-like" platforms to create an ISR/Strike capability that only elite air forces had in the past. Considering the fleeting engagement times of modern combat, the convergence of "find and

In recent years, the Harop loitering munition has proved its lethal combat effectiveness in conflicts in Libya, Syria and Nagorno-Karabakh. The Harop is produced by Israel Aerospace Industries and was one of the most successful loitering munitions used by Azerbaijan during the Second Nagorno-Karabakh War. Israel Aerospace Industries is Israel's major aerospace and aviation manufacturer, producing aerial and astronautic systems for both military and civilian usage. It is completely state-owned by the government of Israel. (IAI image)

strike" provides smaller forces with an important combat multiplier. This capability is particularly useful for expeditionary units. Due to its well-publicized success during the Second Nagorno-Karabakh War, the Harop has become a best-selling system and has been added to the arsenals of Azerbaijan, China, India, South Korea and Turkey. In February 2020, IAI announced it had sold a naval version of the system in three separate deals to an undisclosed customer in Asia for US$100 million. This maritime version has an extended range and will provide a combined ISR and lethal strike capability to a wide variety of naval platforms. It could even be installed on a cargo ship.

The Orbiter 1K

The Aeronautics Orbiter 1K loitering munition, manufactured by the Israel's Aeronautics Defense Systems (aeronautics-sys.com), is also a "kamikaze drone" that was used extensively by Azerbaijan during the Second Nagorno-Karabakh

War. According to Aeronautics, the Orbiter 1K is a lightweight LM designed for missions against non-armored vehicles, equipment and human targets. The Orbiter 1K carries a 3-kilogram (6.6lb) warhead with advanced guidance capabilities, to ensure high precision, lethality and low collateral effects. The Orbiter 1K LM has an endurance of 2.5 hours and a range of 100 kilometers (62 miles). When the Orbiter detects a target, it can autonomously dive to strike the target, self-detonating upon impact. Once launched, it can abort the mission and recover safely to preserve the UAV and avoid expending it unnecessarily. The advanced autonomous mode, and the ability to share real-time intelligence information, made the Orbiter an exceptionally effective LM system during the war.[7]

Implications of UAS, UCAVs and LMs for the future of warfare

With accelerated technological change, the methods of war are evolving, and so are the means to conduct ISR and strike missions. In the decade to come, many ISR systems already fielded will continue in the traditional mode of providing ISR information for other munitions, but an ever-increasing number of platforms will combine ISR and attack. Merging both capabilities into one system creates a powerful combination and this points to a trend for smaller, unmanned platforms with multiple roles. UAVs, which were primarily ISR platforms in the past, are now less expensive, more available, and capable of performing both ISR and strike roles. As we connect more projectiles to a networked "internet of battlespace things," sensors embedded in projectiles will "light up" the surrounding battlespace as they fly to their targets, identifying enemy systems along their route. When this occurs, the battlespace will become transparent.

The battlespace of the next conflict

Warfare is hyper-accelerated. If you move or emit any signal along the electromagnetic spectrum without being hidden, you will be detected in real-time, located precisely, targeted, and killed.

When these systems are connected into a network and form a multi-domain strike capability that leverages the synchronization in time, space and effect with artificial intelligence (AI), the ability for anyone or anything to hide in the battlespace will become much harder, if not impossible. To counter this, new combat systems must be built from the ground up, using passive and active means to mask themselves from these ubiquitous sensors. The merging of ISR and strike capability, when sensors are shooters, represents a capability tested in recent combat and foretells the evolution of the next generation of ISR systems.

Unmanned systems can be designed to help mask forces in the battlespace. Such unmanned systems could jam enemy sensors, send false electromagnetic, acoustic, thermal, and visual signals to multi-domain sensors, act as decoys, and show so many "false positive" indicators that the combination across multiple domains confuses and confounds the enemy's ability to sense and strike. Such a masked force would be nearly invisible to the enemy's high-tech sensors. Masking using unmanned systems may provide the ideal form of one of the extraordinary forces in war that Sun Tzu described in his *Art of War*: "Rushing like the wind; slow-stirring like the forest; consuming like fire; immobile like a mountain. They are as hard to know as shadows. They move like rolling thunder … " (US Army Research Laboratory image)

| Emit anywhere across the Electromagnetic Spectrum | Automatically Targeted | Precision Strike | Destroyed |

This symbolic equation depicts the trends in the development of unmanned aerial systems, loitering munitions, and long-range precision fires linked to ubiquitous sensors. The union of these capabilities will impede ground forces from maneuvering on the battlefield. Ground, air, and space-based sensor networks will detect, identify, and report every movement, electronic emission, and significant variations in the thermal and acoustic spectrum. The precision-strike system will be automated by artificial intelligence. In such a "transparent" battlespace, any system that emits across the electromagnetic spectrum can be seen, targeted in real-time, and rapidly destroyed in a precision strike. (John Antal image)

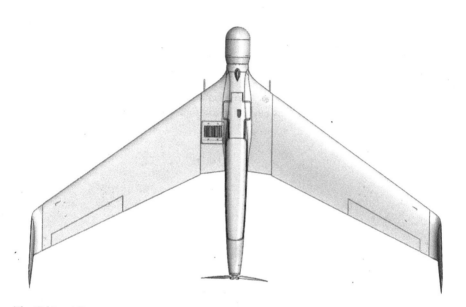

The Orbiter 1K munition unmanned aerial system loitering munition is a "kamikaze" 3-kilogram (6.6lb) fragmentation flying bomb. Azerbaijan purchased Orbiters from Israel's Aeronautics Defense Systems and they performed with devastating effect during the Second Nagorno-Karabakh War. It has a stabilized mini-dual electro-optical and infrared camera that transmits full-motion video. (Aeronautics Group image)

CHAPTER 4

The Drone Advantage

"In the development of air power, one has to look ahead and not backwards and figure out what is going to happen, not too much what has happened."

GENERAL BILLY MITCHELL, IN *WINGED DEFENSE*, 1925

When Azerbaijan attacked on September 27, 2020, both its use of high-technology systems and innovative tactics provided a glimpse of wars to come. The Azerbaijanis executed their version of cross-domain maneuver to win a rapid and decisive victory against a defending and determined adversary. The effective use of unmanned aerial vehicles (UAVs) and loitering munitions (LMs), following Azerbaijan's extensive investment in the latest Turkish and Israeli systems, was stunning. The unrelenting tempo, precision, and lethality of the aerial attacks devastated and demoralized the Armenians and played a definitive role in Azerbaijan's victory. Hikmet Hajiyev, foreign policy adviser to Azerbaijan's President Ilham Aliyev, reported in an interview to the *Financial Times* on October 26, 2020:

> What we see is that there was a factor of invincibility that Armenia had tried to propagate over many years ... but they relied too much on old military doctrine and thinking: tanks, heavy artillery and fortifications. It simply reminded us of the Second World War ... Instead, mobile forces, drone technology and a modern approach has been applied by us.

The unmanned systems did not win the war by themselves, and UAVs have been over-hyped in many press accounts of the war, but the impact of the high-definition full motion video (FMV) provided by top-attack systems categorized this conflict as "the war of the drones." The Azerbaijanis used the secure FMV capabilities of their systems to enhance sensor-shooter integration, to obtain battle damage assessment, and for propaganda to win the information war. In these aspects, especially the use of secure tactical FMV video and data links, the conflict is a harbinger for wars to come.

Sensor-Shooter integration

The first phase of the Azerbaijani effort was to employ their newly acquired high-tech UAVs and LMs, in addition to conventional artillery and rockets, to take down the Armenian air defense and command and control (C2) network. They did this in the first weeks of the war. Armenian air defense, made up of older Russian-made systems, could not stop the UAV and LM attacks. Even when the air defense systems were operating, the aerial top-attack weapons penetrated the airspace and knocked out the defenders. Azerbaijan used a wide variety of UAVs during the war and the most effective and notorious were the Turkish-made Bayraktar TB2, the Israeli-made Harop (see previous chapter for descriptions of both), and the fully autonomous Israeli-made SkyStriker (Elbit Systems). The electro-optical sensors on the most sophisticated UAVs and LMs used by Azerbaijan are state of the art infrared and low-light high-definition television cameras that deliver secure tactical video reconnaissance, surveillance, and targeting data. During the war, the TB2 operated as an attack platform and as the "eye in the sky" for Azerbaijani forces to identify and designate targets for other UAVs, LMs, artillery, rockets, and smart anti-tank guided missiles (ATGM), such as the Israeli-made Spike ATGM system.

While the TB2 identified Armenian forces in the designated strike zone, LMs circled autonomously overhead, automatically verifying their targets and then diving on to their victims to detonate their 23-kilogram (50lb) warheads in a kamikaze-like attack. Prior to launch, the Harops were programmed to

The Bayraktar TB2 uses an Aselsan Common Aperture Targeting system for electro-optical reconnaissance, surveillance, and targeting. Low-light and infrared high-definition cameras generate an unblinking eye of the battlespace. The Azerbaijanis used the full motion video capability of the TB2 to great advantage in the Second Nagorno-Karabakh War. (Wiki Commons, Bayhaluk photo)

autonomously fly to a pre-defined strike zone. Once there, they loitered and the human operator selected one LM for target search and attack, while the others were monitored periodically. The vital component is the HD camera system which allows the operator to gain situation awareness of the battlespace and direct the LM to attack designated targets.

Battle damage assessment

Once Azerbaijan knocked out enough Armenian air defense and C2 to achieve air superiority over designated strike zones, the UAV and LM effort concentrated on targeting artillery, tanks, and infantry units in bloody top-attacks. Since the modern UAVs and LMs contained both situation awareness and weapons capability in the same platforms, the Azerbaijanis could accurately count their kills. Using the FMV from both UAVs and LMs to understand how many Armenian systems were destroyed or disabled helped guide combined arms assaults that led to the capture of terrain that dominated the major highways linking Nagorno-Karabakh through mountain passes to Armenia. Once the Azerbaijanis secured these vital roads, it placed the Armenians in Nagorno-Karabakh on the horns of a dilemma: fight to the death or surrender. Desperate to save their forces, Armenia proposed a ceasefire. Azerbaijan rejected the initial overtures as their ground forces moved to capture the major cities and decisive terrain in Nagorno-Karabakh. Only once its objectives were achieved did Azerbaijan agree to a ceasefire. In a de facto surrender, Armenia accepted Azerbaijan's terms on November 10, 2020, and withdrew from territories surrounding Nagorno-Karabakh. Throughout the war, UAV and LM videos, bolstered by robust and secure tactical video feeds, provided the Azerbaijanis with superior situation awareness.

Oryx Blog

During the Second Nagorno-Karabakh War, drone footage from Armenian and Azerbaijan systems was catalogued in almost real-time by military analysists Stijn Mitzer and Joost Oliemans on their Oryx blog, which collects very accurate, open-source, intelligence on current military conflicts around the world. During the war they listed destroyed and captured equipment of both sides and corroborated this with images from full-motion video footage from actual drone strikes.

Information war

Azerbaijan, with the aid of Turkey, planned and prepared a high-tech conflict against Armenia for at least a decade prior to September 2020. Part of this strategy involved winning the information war. This effort was designed to confuse and demoralize Armenian forces and break the will of the Armenian population. The high-definition video footage of the precision drone attacks depicted burning tanks and devastating explosions among groups of Armenian soldiers. The Azerbaijanis used these in countless propaganda films on the internet and social media platforms. Armenians viewed this footage and feared for their soldiers. In this propaganda effort, the Azerbaijani message was loud and clear: "We are winning. We will bring you death from above with our drones and you can't stop us." As Armenian losses surged and their lines continued to fall back, morale suffered.

The Harop loitering missile is an electro-optically guided attack weapon. Harops are launched from ground-based launchers and controlled via a two-way data link for "human on the loop" or "human out of the loop" operation, using its anti-radar homing system. It is used to attack high-value targets, including full mission capabilities, from search, through attack and up to battle damage assessment. Combining characteristics of a missile and a UAV, Harop enables effective mission execution without relying on other external systems for targeting and mission intelligence. If a target is not engaged, the drone will return to base. The Harop can be launched from a truck with as many as 12 weapons per vehicle. (IAI image)

Courage is useless in the face of educated bullets, and the Azerbaijani top-attack munitions hit their targets with brilliant accuracy. Leveraging the power of real-time video capture by unmanned systems to win the information war is relatively new and the Azerbaijani's played this hand skillfully.

Learning from History

As the 1973 Yom Kippur War was studied as an example of modern combined arms operations during the late 20th century, the Second Nagorno-Karabakh War holds lessons in the dynamic clash between attack and defense, the use of technology, and conduct of cross-domain maneuver for today. The increasing "democratization of technology," whereby high-tech weaponry such as UAVs and LMs become available to all, and the secure tactical video produced by these weapons used as a powerful propaganda tool, has serious implications for Western military forces. The battlespace is now transparent and there is nowhere to hide. As with the Yom Kippur War, the question on the minds of many Western military leaders should be whether the combat units of NATO would fare any better than the Armenians under the Azerbaijani whirlwind? Has NATO fielded the integrated air defense capability to counter UAV and LM assaults? How many NATO units have recently trained against UAV and LM swarm attacks? How will NATO integrate the command-and-control cross-domain capabilities of 29 multinational, multi-service UAV systems? These questions demand answers.

Tackling this challenge should start with a detailed study of the Second Nagorno-Karabakh War to derive lessons learned, and then transform those lessons into updated doctrine, training, and equipment. One of the key lessons is the use of secure tactical video-equipped UAVs and LMs to enhance sensor-shooter integration, raise situation awareness through battle damage assessment, and to win the information war. When the next conflict between peer-competitors occurs, the side that fails to learn the lessons of the Second Nagorno-Karabakh War will find themselves at a significant strategic and tactical disadvantage they may not be able to overcome.

Unmanned aerial systems are a growing challenge in today's battlespace. Operating in swarms, these systems can be even more deadly. The US Army has selected Northrop Grumman to develop and integrate a directed energy prototype solution on a Stryker combat vehicle to better protect highly mobile front-line units. (Northrop Grumman image)

CHAPTER 5

Smashing the Drone Swarm: The Art of Interdicting Unmanned Aerial Systems

"A strong defense against Unmanned Aerial System Threats (CUAS) requires a comprehensive, end-to-end approach ... an integrated, layered solution across the kill chain."

NORTHRUP GRUMMAN CORPORATION

On a clear night with a full moon, sometime before 4am on September 14, 2019, twenty delta-winged, Iranian unmanned aerial vehicles (UAVs) fanned out in a wide formation, flying fast over empty desert terrain. The UAVs flew low to avoid Saudi radar detection and only gained altitude during the very last minutes of their flight. As they neared their objective, the Aramco Abqaiq oil facility, they climbed and then dove into the critical refinery infrastructure, striking their targets with pin-point accuracy. At nearly the same time, four cruise missiles hit the remote oil complex at Khurais, 212 kilometers (132 miles) to the southwest. Explosions rocked the ground as the sky above Abqaiq and Khurais lit up with fire. As the conflagrations raged, Riyadh's oil production was temporarily cut in half and oil prices soared 20 percent. The Iranians coupled their attack with a disinformation campaign that the weapons used in the raid had come from their Houthi proxy forces in Yemen, but the wreckage of the suicide UAVs salvaged after the fires were identified by Saudi Ministry of Defense officials as "Iranian Delta Wave UAVs." Regardless of who was responsible for the strike, the Saudis had just experienced what Israeli air and missile defense expert Uzi Rubin called "a kind of 'Pearl Harbor' attack," using a swarm of low-altitude unmanned aerial systems (UAS), loitering munitions (LMs) and high-speed cruise missiles.

The attack on the Saudi oil complexes highlighted the urgent require-ment to have robust, multilayered, counter-unmanned aerial system (CUAS) defenses. A UAS is the complete package that consists of the unmanned aircraft, a payload, a radio receiver as a means of control and data transfer, and a human operator, whereas the UAV is simply an unmanned aircraft. The use of such systems to provide a targeting sensor network for Russian proxy forces in Ukraine, and their use with explosive payloads in Syria, provide additional examples of the hybrid use of these new weapons in modern war. Today, the proliferation of cheap and inexpensive UAS technology provides nearly any aggressor with a hip-pocket air force at its disposal. Imagine a swarm of hundreds of drones attacking Saudi facilities, not just 20 UAVs. Defending against this threat is a challenge military forces around the world are struggling to deal with. From commercial systems to more expensive and capable arrangements, there is a growing and increasingly deadly range of threats that must be countered.

As UAS technology is complemented with artificial intelligence (AI), the future battlespace promises to be awash with swarms of faster, smarter, fully autonomous, and more lethal systems. An effective CUAS solution in these circumstances must rapidly detect, locate, track, identify and defeat the threat. Detection can involve a range of means, including the use of radio frequency analyzers, radar, optical sensors, and acoustic systems. Detection is increasingly difficult as UAVs become stealthier and so small that they blend into the background clutter. Once detected, interdicting a UAS attack can be accomplished by either a "soft-kill" or "hard-kill" approach. A soft kill employs an electronic warfare (EW), high-power microwave (HPM) generating an electromagnetic pulse (EMP), or a cyberwarfare system to interdict or control the UAV. Hard kill involves the physical interruption of a UAV's ability to fly and continue its mission by physically destroying it. Hard kill systems usually employ kinetic munitions. Combining these methods, either with separate systems or having several methods embedded in a single system, provides a layered and more effective CUAS defense. The best CUAS tactics apply a multi-layered approach. The CUAS fight is won when the opponent's systems are disrupted, paralyzed, or destroyed.

UAV Classification according to the US Department of Defense (DoD)				
Category	Size	Max Gross Takeoff Weight	Normal Operating Altitude	Airspeed
Group 1	Small	0–20 lb	<1,200 ft AGL	<100 knots
Group 2	Medium	21–55 lb	<3,500 ft AGL	<250 knots
Group 3	Large	<1,320 lb	<18,000 ft MSL	<250 knots
Group 4	Larger	>1,320 lb	<18,000 ft MSL	Any
Group 5	Largest	>1,320 lb	>18,000 ft MSL	Any

AGL = Above Ground Level

MSL = Mean Sea Level

Note: If the UAS has even one characteristic of the next level, it is classified in that level.

Source: *Eyes of the Army: U.S. Army Roadmap for UAS 2010–2035*

The eXpeditionary Mobile Air Defense Integrated System by Ascent Vision Technologies, a CACI (Consolidated Analysis Center, Incorporated) company, is a portable full-spectrum, counter small unmanned aircraft system capability that detects, locates, tracks, identifies, and defeats single or multiple small unmanned aerial system threats. It provides reliable protection against Group 1, 2, and 3 systems. (AVT image)

Soft-kill systems

The eXpeditionary Mobile Air Defense Integrated System (X-MADIS) by Ascent Vision Technologies (AVT), headquartered in Belgrade, Montana, USA, is an example of a soft-kill fixed site or mobile vehicle mounted system designed primarily to counter small (Group 1) and medium (Group 2) UAS. The X-MADIS uses an S-band, pulse Doppler radar; cutting-edge multi-sensor optics; and a powerful EW jammer to provide 360-degree protection against medium and small UAS (sUAS). The mobile system is light enough to mount in a pick-up truck, can operate on the move and provides protection against UASs (Group 1) up to 3.5 kilometers (2 miles), medium-sized (Group 2) UASs out to 15 kilometers (9 miles), aircraft detection up to 25 kilometers (15.5 miles) and helicopter detection range up to 30 kilometers (18.6 miles). According to AVT, this CUAS "has an integrated, all-threat tactical air surveillance radar, gyro-stabilized optical sensor (EO [Electro-Optical] and MWIR [Medium-Wavelength Infra-Red] imagery), C2 interface and Electronic Warfare System, to provide a complete 'soft-kill' solution to combat the growing threat of hostile sUAS, and near-peer air threats." AVT states X-MADIS can detect, identify and interdict all classes of UASs including nano, micro and mini-size systems including a UAS swarm. In 2019, AVT was awarded a contract in excess of US$23 million to deliver a full suite of X-MADIS-equipped vehicles to the United States Air Force.

Armenian Electronic Warfare (EW) Systems Deployed to Soft-Kill UAVs

The Russians are developing layered air defense networks to defeat drones. One Russian CUAS system that has been used in combat and exported to several countries is the Repellent CUAS system. This soft-kill system works by jamming and disrupting the drone's signal communications within the 200–6,000 MHz frequency band at a distance of up to 30 km. During the Second Nagorno-Karabakh War, however, the Armenians deployed the Repellent system with dubious results. In a radio address on December 8, 2020, Armenian Prime Minister Nikol Pashinyan reported that the Russian-made EW systems, such as the "Repellent," simply did not work, but said the Osa-AK, "hit many targets during the war." During the war, Azerbiajani TB2 was credited with destroying a "Repellent" CUAS system.[1] Russian experts scoffed at this report saying that Pashinyan was trying to shift the responsibility for Armenia's defeat.

Some tactical situations require a soldier to possess a shoulder-fired solution. The DroneDefender is an example of a cost-effective, soft-kill, rifle-like, directed-energy CUAS system. DroneDefender was developed by Battelle researchers to meet an urgent need of the US military. It was so impressive that the technology was purchased from Battelle by Dedrone in 2019. DroneDefender is a point-and-shoot system that can interdict a hostile UAS within a 400-meter (1300 feet) radius and uses radio pulses to disable the global positioning satellite signal or ISM (industrial, scientific and medical) radio bands, creating electromagnetic interference and disrupting radio communication control. According to Battelle, "These radio pulses interrupt the UAV's communication system, either forcing the drone to hover, return to its point of origin, or descend slowly as it prepares to land. Because the weapon jams communication with the nearby operator, the DroneDefender also can prevent detonation and other remote functions."

Soft-Kill jammers, such as the DroneDefender system, provide a means for individual soldiers to stop sUAS attacks. Soldiers from the 1st Squadron, 3rd Cavalry Regiment, operate the DroneDefender during a counter-unmanned aerial system drill while deployed to Iraq, October 30, 2018. The 3rd Cavalry Regiment was deployed in support of Operation *Inherent Resolve*, working with the Iraqi Security Forces and Coalition partners to defeat ISIS in areas of Iraq and Syria. (US Army photo)

Another soft-kill system, the High-Power Electro-Magnetics (HPEM) CUAS system, developed by German-based Diehl Defense, interdicts UAVs by generating a blast of EMP that renders the UAV inoperable. The system is short range but scalable. Using the same general method, Lockheed Martin was awarded a contract by the United States Army in November 2018 for a flying HPM soft-kill system that will fry, blind, or jam the electronics of an enemy UAS. Lockheed Martin may elect to place the HPM payload on their Stalker XE UAS. According to Lockheed Martin, "Stalker XE is an operationally proven, small, and silent, UAS with a digital backbone that allows for rapid plug and play … and is in use by Special Forces around the world." Flying over a swarm of enemy UAS, a friendly UAS with a HPM payload could disrupt the swarm.

Hard-kill systems

Research is being conducted to bring high-energy lasers to the battlespace for CUAS. Under an initiative from the United States Army Rapid Capabilities and Critical Technologies Office, and a contract from Kord Technologies, Northrop Grumman is building and integrating a suite of advanced sensors, consisting of target acquisition and tracking, a 50-kilowatt class laser system, and a battle-tested command-and-control system, on an Army Stryker combat vehicle. The effort will culminate in a competitive performance checkout leading to a live-fire range demonstration that will inform medium–short range air defense requirements.

In 2018, the US Army deployed a five-kilowatt Mobile Expeditionary High Energy Laser on several Stryker armored vehicles and tested them against Group 1 unmanned aerial systems. The *Army Times* reported that Staff Sergeant Eric Davis, a fire support non-commissioned officer with 4th Division Artillery, 4th Infantry Division, recalled at the time: "It was extremely efficient. I was able to bring them (threat UAVs) down as (fast as) they were able to bring them up."

DroneBullet is another example of a hard-kill system that uses a UAS to kill a UAS. DroneBullet, developed by a Vancouver, Canada, company, AerialX, is a kamikaze UAS that is, according to Noam Kenig, the CEO, a "hybrid between a missile and a quadcopter … It can track objects autonomously and will even work out exactly where to hit its target, depending on its speed and whether [its target is] a quadcopter or fixed-wing drone." The DroneBullet weighs only 910 grams, can fly for four kilometers (2.5 miles), and can reach

Installed on a Stryker armored vehicle, the Mobile Expeditionary High Energy Laser was very successful at interdicting UAVs during a test in 2018. The US Army intends to field-test two different types of high-energy lasers in 2022: a 50-kilowatt weapon to defeat enemy drones and incoming artillery rockets, and a 300-kilowatt laser system that could potentially shoot down cruise missiles. (US Army photo)

a speed of about 190 knots in its final dive. DroneBullet contains no explosive warhead and destroys its intended target using kinetic energy.

Layered counter-swarm systems

Defeating UAS swarms requires a layered approach, but the backbone of the defense must be a system with range, lethality, and plenty of shots. Raytheon's high energy laser (HEL) system, paired with Raytheon's multi-spectral targeting system of sensors and HPM CUAS, has demonstrated a layered defense that has worked in several tests. In 2019, a Raytheon-built CUAS microwave system and a HEL system worked together to bring down dozens of small drones during an exercise conducted at White Sands Missile Range in New Mexico. The target drones were flying both alone and in swarms. Mounted on a small, all-terrain, militarized vehicle, the Raytheon HEL detected, identified, tracked and engaged drones with its laser. Working with the HEL, Raytheon's

HPM CUAS used microwave energy to disrupt the UAS guidance systems. High-power microwave operators can focus the beam to bring down UAS swarms. If there is a consistent power supply, the HEL and HPM systems can complement each other to provide effective CUAS protection. "The speed and low cost per engagement of directed energy is revolutionary in protecting our troops against drones," said Dr. Thomas Bussing, Raytheon Advanced Missile Systems vice-president. "After decades of research and investment, we believe these advanced directed energy applications will soon be ready for the battlespace." The results of the test demonstrate that the system works and is ready for fielding. Once deployed, powering these systems and protecting them from the more common battlespace threats, such as missile attack and indirect artillery fires, must be a priority.

Another example of a next-generation a soft-kill system is one designed by Northrup-Grumman Defense, which partnered with Epirus, to develop a High Power Microwave CUAS solution. Called the Leonidas, referencing the stand of the 300 Spartans at Thermopylae in 480 B.C. against hordes of enemies,

Raytheon Corporation has developed a layered CUAS defense using a high-power microwave system working with a high energy laser system that successfully brought down swarms of unmanned aerial systems in recent live-fire tests. The directed energy system emits an adjustable energy beam that, when aimed at airborne targets, such as drones, renders them unable to fly. (US Army photo)

this HPM weapon utilizes a solid-state design that delivers unparalleled digital "beamforming" and instant engagement to counter multiple UAS simultaneously. Northrup-Grumman claims that Leonidas can defeat a wide range of UAS, including swarm attacks, in a wide area of the battlespace with sweeps of its digital beam technology. Leonidas is designed to protect forward operating bases, fixed sites, and maneuver forces against hostile UAS and can be fully integrated with Northrop Grumman's forward area air defense command and control system used by the US Army.

High Power Microwave Weapons (HPM)

HPM use electromagnetic radiation in the microwave band to disrupt, degrade or destroy electronic systems or circuits. HPM weapons shoot a beam of energy at the "speed of light" to knock out UAS. HPM weapons operate from 500 MHz to 3 GHz, but newer systems are extending the power to 100 GHz. Their biggest drawback is short range and the requirement to supply the weapon system with megawatts of electrical power.

The future of the CUAS

As the drone attack on the Saudi oil fields proved, the use of unmanned systems is changing how wars are waged. The UAS market reflects this trend and Fortune Business Insights, a leading publisher of financial market information, reported in January 2020 that the military drone market size was US$7.93 billion in 2018; it is projected to reach US$21.76 billion by 2026, a 64 percent increase in just six years. The CUAS market is currently less than the UAS market, but investments in the former are accelerating and are projected to be in the US$1–2 billion range by 2025. According to a new report titled *The DOD's CUAS Strategy* by the Institute for Defense and Government Advancement, the US military alone spent $900 million on CUAS solutions in 2019 and intended to spend more in 2020. Much of this money will be used to develop layered systems designed to defeat swarms of UAVs. In October 2016, the US Department of Defense, the Strategic Capabilities Office, partnering with Naval Air Systems Command, successfully demonstrated one of the world's largest micro-drone swarms at China Lake,

California. The swarm consisted of 103 Perdix drones launched from three F/A-18 Super Hornets. The micro-drones demonstrated advanced swarm behaviors such as collective decision-making, adaptive formation flying and self-healing. As the offensive capability of unmanned aerial systems continues to improve, the need for a CUAS capability becomes self-evident.

The Russian Army and Chinese People's Liberation Army (PLA) are also very interested in unmanned aerial systems and swarming. In a November 7, 2019, article, Izvestia reported "The fighters of the Russian army for the first time worked out the elements of the 'war of the future'—the actions of UAV strike groups." The article went on to say that the Zhukovsky Air Force Engineering Academy had developed a concept, titled "Flock-93," which involves a swarm of more than one hundred kamikaze drones, each carrying more than 1–2 kilograms (2.2–4.4lb) of explosives, used to attack high-value targets such as convoys, command posts, and air defense systems. Swarms of hundreds of UAVs have not yet been seen in combat, but the Russians and PLA are testing such tactics. In 2018, the China Electronics Technology Group Corporation and Tsinghua University released a video of a swarm zooming in improvised, network-generated flight patterns. In October 2019, the PLA put on a display of its latest, high-end UAS during the Nation Day Parade. As UASs gain more range and AI-driven autonomy, their ability to think independently and operate in swarms of hundreds of UAVs will create a game-changing threat. Just as air defense was crucial to the success of combined operations in the 20th century, CUAS operations and smashing the swarm are vital to surviving and winning in today's battlespace.

The US military is adapting to meet the challenges of drone warfare. 1st Lt. Taylor Barefoot, a low altitude air defense officer with Marine Medium Tiltrotor Squadron 163 (Reinforced), 11th Marine Expeditionary Unit, programs a counter-unmanned aircraft system on a Light Marine Air Defense Integrated System (LMADIS) during a predeployment training exercise at Marine Corps Air Ground Combat Center Twentynine Palms, Calif., Nov. 13, 2018. The LMADIS is a maneuverable, ground based system, mounted to a Polaris MRZR that can detect, identify and defeat drones with electronic attack. (U.S. Marine Corps photo by Lance Cpl. Dalton S. Swanbeck)

The range of sUAS can be increased by employing recent advances in hydrogen fuel cell technology. Three examples fly at Edwards Air Force Base, California, August 21, 2019. Most small vehicles like these are battery powered. Hydrogen fuel cells can extend range and endurance, enabling more effective swarming tactics. According to US Army Training and Doctrine Command's Pamphlet 525-92, "Unmanned systems, including advanced battlefield robotic systems acting both autonomously and as part of a wider trend in man-machine teaming, will account for a significant percentage of a combatant force. Swarms of small, cheap, scalable, and disposable unmanned systems will be used both offensively and defensively, creating targeting dilemmas for sophisticated, expensive defensive systems. Swarming systems on the future battlefield will include not only unmanned aerial systems but also swarms across multiple domains with the self-organizing, self-reconstituting, autonomous, ground, maritime (sub and surface), and subterranean unmanned systems." (US Air Force photo, Staff Sergeant Rachel Simones)

CHAPTER 6

The Need for Power: Batteries versus Fuel Cells for Unmanned Aerial Vehicles

"Drones and most likely drone swarms are something you're going to see on a future battlefield."

GENERAL JOHN MURRAY, COMMANDER, US ARMY FUTURES COMMAND

The modern weapons of war are thirsty for electrical power. Hybrid engines and all-electric motors promise to be the future of commercial and military systems, but due to the cost of replacing entire fleets of vehicles, and the reliability of petrol and diesel engines, most military forces will be tied to internal combustion technology for many years. Small Unmanned Aerial Vehicles (UAVs), however, offer an exception. These weapons are playing an increasingly critical role in combat operations and are mostly powered by batteries. For these systems, staying in the air and operating for hours, rather than minutes, can be the difference between mission success and failure. Extending the flight time of small UAVs, therefore, is becoming a priority. There are two primary means of providing electrical power for these machines: batteries that store electrical energy or fuel cells that generate electrical power.

Batteries

Today, Lithium-ion (Li-ion) batteries power nearly every rechargeable device on the market, and they are also the most common battery used by small UAVs. According to the Clean Energy Institute, at the University of Washington, a Li-ion battery:

... is an advanced battery technology that uses lithium ions as a key component of its electrochemistry. During a discharge cycle, lithium atoms in the anode are ionized and separated from their electrons. The lithium ions move from the anode and pass through the electrolyte until they reach the cathode, where they recombine with their electrons and electrically neutralize. The lithium ions are small enough to be able to move through a micro-permeable separator between the anode and cathode.[1]

The advantage of Li-ion batteries is that they have the highest energy density per weight of any other battery. In addition, they are commercially available and are the key power source for electric road vehicles.

Elon Musk, the CEO of Tesla, has pledged to develop improved Li-ion batteries for his electric cars. In September 2020, he promised to automate production of his newly designed "tab-less" 4680 Li-ion battery cells. Battery "tabs" are metallic components welded onto battery electrodes. With the new tab-less design, the electrons inside the battery experience less heat and resistance. According to Tesla's 4680 patent:

> Current cells use a jelly-roll design in which the cathode, anode, and separators are rolled together and have a cathode tab and an anode tab to connect to the positive and negative terminals of the cell can. The path of the current necessarily travels through these tabs to connectors on the outside of the battery cell. However, ohmic resistance is increased with distance when current must travel all the way along the cathode or anode to the tab and out of the cell. Furthermore, because the tabs are additional components, they increase costs and present manufacturing challenges.[2]

The new 4680 tab-less battery will provide five times the energy, six times the power, and 16 percent greater range than the battery currently used in Tesla cars. This new high-density 4680 cell is projected to cost less than current batteries because of Musk's plans for streamline manufacturing and

Improved batteries that can hold a strong charge for longer durations will increase the range of small unmanned aerial systems. Tesla's future 4680 battery cell is intended to have six times more power, five times more energy, and 16 percent more range. (Tesla image)

large-scale production. This is good news for Tesla customers, as it will reduce the price of electric cars, and the military. As Li-ion batteries improve in the commercial sector, they will become more available and less expensive to power military systems. The 4680 battery, or similar designs, could increase range and capability for small UAVs. This new battery technology, however, is still years away. There are thousands of UAVs military forces need to upgrade right now, not in 2023 or 2024. To keep small UAVs flying and operating longer, we need an alternative power source.

Fuel cells

To extend endurance, hydrogen fuel cells provide an immediate solution. Fuel cell technology can be two to three times more efficient than internal combustion engines and generate three times more energy density than Li-ion batteries. Hydrogen fuel cells convert hydrogen and oxygen into water and, in the process, produce electricity and heat as long as fuel is supplied. A fuel cell consists of a negative electrode (or anode) and a positive electrode (or cathode) sandwiched around an electrolyte. A small hydrogen fuel tank attached to the UAV provides the hydrogen while oxygen is pulled from the atmosphere. The problem with fuel cells is the availability of pure hydrogen gas. You can't just pull it from the surrounding air. Although hydrogen may

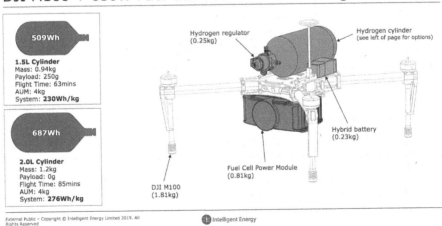

DJI M100 + 650W Fuel Cell Power Module configurations

509Wh

1.5L Cylinder
Mass: 0.94kg
Payload: 250g
Flight Time: 63mins
AUM: 4kg
System: **230Wh/kg**

687Wh

2.0L Cylinder
Mass: 1.2kg
Payload: 0g
Flight Time: 85mins
AUM: 4kg
System: **276Wh/kg**

Hydrogen regulator
(0.25kg)

Hydrogen cylinder
(see left of page for options)

Hybrid battery
(0.23kg)

Fuel Cell Power Module
(0.81kg)

DJI M100
(1.81kg)

Intelligent Energy

Intelligent Energy is a world-leader in hydrogen fuel cell power for small UAVs. The diagram above shows the fuel cell configuration for one of their UAVs. (Intelligent Energy diagram)

be the most common element found on earth, it is difficult and expensive to capture and store. To be useful, hydrogen is pressurized in steel tanks.

Several companies have made hydrogen fuel cells for small UAVs that significantly extend range and outperform battery systems. One company, Ballard Unmanned Systems, a Southborough, Massachusetts-based company purchased by Honeywell in late 2020, launched a turnkey hydrogen fuel cell UAV configuration that can be applied to most existing small UAVs. This system enables small UAVs to fly approximately three times longer than with the leading battery systems. Another company, Intelligent Energy, produces a hydrogen fuel cell for small UAVs that extends flight time from minutes to hours and allows the UAV to carry a heavier payload. In 2019, Intelligent Energy partnered with South Korean liquid hydrogen specialist MetaVista to create a hydrogen fuel cell that powered a UAV to break the world record for the longest flight time (12 hours, 7 minutes, and 22 seconds). The MetaVista team used a 6-liter (203 fl oz) liquid hydrogen cylinder and Intelligent Energy's 800W Fuel Cell Power Module to power the UAV.

Hydrogen Fuel Cell for sUAS

Hydrogen fuel cell technology enables small drones to carry more payload and to fly three times longer than batteries with equivalent output. With the latest hydrogen fuel cell systems, sUAS operators can refuel or swap hydrogen tanks in minutes, enabling more time in the air.

Small UAVs will increasingly play an important role in future conflicts by providing both offensive and defensive capabilities. They will be used to gather intelligence, surveillance, and reconnaissance information; or operate in autonomous, networked swarms to attack targets beyond visual line of sight; or defend critical systems to defeat enemy UAVs. With the limitations of current batteries, and substantial improvements still very much in the future, Ballard and Intelligent Systems have proven hydrogen fuel cells provide a viable, and affordable, solution to extend the capabilities of small UAVs. For increased endurance, especially for machines that need to operate for extended periods or conduct beyond visual line of sight operations, fuel cells are the answer.

"...combat-effective drones will proliferate. These drones would not be very complex systems, like the ones used by the United States, but 'good enough' systems that could impact the regional conflicts. Therefore, they will be part of future warfare."
Oğuzhan Çakır, "Interview with Dr. Çağlar Kurç The Second Nagorno-Karabakh War and UCAVs," *Political Reflections*, July–September 2021. p.34.

In the largest drone battle in history, the 2020 Second Nagorno-Karabakh War, Azerbaijan destroyed Armenian forces and won a decisive victory primarily with unmanned systems. (Photo taken from Azerbaijan Ministry of Defense video)

CHAPTER 7

Training and Equipping for the Coming Drone Wars

"Commanders must plan, prepare, execute, and assess their units' skills against the threat environment in which the units will conduct operations. Passive air defense, combined arms for air defense and counter-reconnaissance tasks training should be an integral part of the units' pre-deployment CUAS training and practices."

US ARMY COUNTER-UNMANNED AIRCRAFT SYSTEM TECHNIQUES, ATP 3-01.81, 2017

Warfare is changing and training is not keeping pace. Recent combat actions in Libya, Syria, and especially in Nagorno-Karabakh in 2020, demonstrated the value of unmanned systems in conducting precision strikes. According to confirmed drone video footage, during the recent Nagorno-Karabakh War, Azerbaijan destroyed at least 1,021 Armenian military systems with unmanned aerial systems (UASs). These included air defense and electronic warfare systems, tanks, howitzers and trucks. In addition, UASs killed hundreds of troops occupying dug-in positions. Azerbaijan's UASs and loitering munitions were difficult to detect and hard to destroy with traditional air defense systems. This level of destruction by unmanned systems was unprecedented in the history of war. One Armenian soldier said "We could not hide, and we could not fight back."

As militaries around the world comprehend the lessons from these recent conflicts, they are scrambling to purchase and field their own UAS precision strike capabilities and Counter Unmanned Aerial Systems (CUAS). New systems alone are not the answer; the solution involves both equipment and training. The urgent requirement to train personnel in both offensive and defensive UAS operations using actual systems is costly and time-consuming. Evolving immersive training technologies, such as Extended Reality (XR), provide an immediate, effective and less expensive training venue.

XR is the conglomeration of three realities: virtual reality (VR), augmented reality (AR) and mixed reality (MR). Integrating XR into live (soldiers training on real systems), virtual (soldiers operating simulated systems), and constructive (soldiers placed in a manual or computer-driven simulation to learn specific tactics, techniques or procedures) training can offer a viable, cost-effective means to train forces for offensive and defensive UAS warfare.

Immersive Technologies

VR   Virtual reality places the user into a computer-simulated world.

AR   Augmented reality overlays information onto the actual world.

MR   Mixed reality mixes VR and AR into reality to interact with physical and digital objects in real-time.

XR   Extended reality converges VR, AR, and MR into one term.

Virtual reality systems

Virtual reality places the user in a computer-generated virtual world. It has rapidly evolved in commercial gaming and education over the past two decades and VR systems are used to train warfighters, units and staff. One example is Virtual Battlespace 3 (VBS3) developed by Bohemia Interactive Simulations. VBS3 is a comprehensive, desktop training package used by NATO forces that is based on commercial video game technology. The latest version is VBS4, which can connect to a VR headset, such as the Oculus Quest, to create an immersive training environment. Oculus Quest, developed by Facebook, is a stand-alone device that runs on the Android operating system and retails for about US$400. The US Army and many NATO countries use Oculus headsets for immersive training. By adapting the existing VBS4 software development kit, trainers can create immersive scenarios, such as what occurred in the Nagorno-Karabakh War, to raise tactical awareness of the emergent UAS threat through adaptive, repetitive training in both offensive and CUAS scenarios.

Augmented reality

AR also provides an available and inexpensive method of training for UAS warfare. It overlays digital information onto the real world and allows users to place virtual objects. This enables nearly any smart device with a camera and the proper software to function as an AR training tool. An example of AR is the "Call for Fire" application produced by Simulation Training Group and offered on the Apple App Store for US$1.99. It trains the user to call for artillery fire. Creating a similar AR "app" to provide for the placement of digital UAS targets on to actual, geospecific terrain would permit a warfighter to engage enemy UAS with CUAS weapons. These digital targets could move at realistic speeds and represent individual UAS systems or swarms. This entire exercise, conducted at the cost of a smartphone or tablet, software, and battery power, would enable warfighters to train repetitively to gain mastery of critical cognitive tasks, thus transforming commercial off-the-shelf (COTS) hardware, with specially designed software, into powerful, low-cost AR UAS training devices.

Mixed reality

MR combines VR and AR into an environment that enables the user to interact with both the virtual and physical world in real-time. The US Army is rapidly fielding an MR capability called the Integrated Visual Augmentation System (IVAS).

The US Army Chief of Staff, General James C. McConville, described IVAS as "cutting edge technology, that will transform the way we train Soldiers, and the way Soldiers operate in combat." IVAS uses MR to provide soldiers with enhanced visual and command and control awareness. Developed by Microsoft using their Hololens2 technology, IVAS is both a tactical goggle and a training device. "HoloLens is essentially a Windows 10 computer that you wear on your face," said Mark Valentine, director of the Army team at Microsoft in November 2019, "but the display methodology is not a screen. It's now a mixed-reality portal to the real world." Using MR, digital holograms, representing enemy UAVs, could appear in the sky during live training. With the proper software, IVAS could engage warfighters in realistic UAS and CUAS battle scenarios.

Extended reality

The key to training in XR is the development of military training software to run on COTS devices. VBS3 software is already available and, with targeted software modifications, could rapidly fill a portion of the UAS and CUAS training gap using VR. The next priority must be to develop immersive UAS and CUAS operations software for AR and MR devices. The US Army recognized the need for agile software development and established the first-of-its kind Army Software Factory in Austin, Texas, at the US Army's

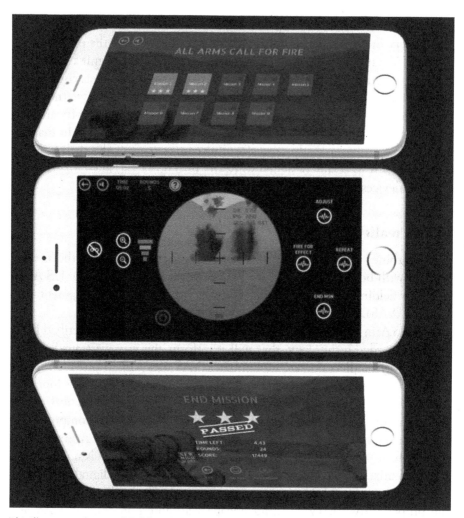

This illustration depicts a "Call for Fire" trainer developed for smart phones and tablets. With minor upgrades, apps like this could turn every smartphone or tablet into an augmented reality CUAS trainer. Simple and inexpensive augmented reality apps could be developed for smartphone and tablet devises to depict AR "drone" attacks and used in virtual or live training. (Simulation Training Group photo)

Futures Command, in mid-2021. In addition, the US Army recently awarded a contract to Octo, an artificial intelligence and internet technologies solutions company, and QinetiQ, the British multinational defense technology company headquartered in Farnborough, Hampshire, to provide machine and deep learning support for IVAS. These two new efforts will provide a robust software development base to help address the shortfalls in UAS and CUAS training.

Soldiers of the US Army's 82nd Airborne Division train with integrated visual augmentation system headsets in March 2021. The core engine of the system is a version of Microsoft's HoloLens. This configuration, maximized for command and control, could become a valuable tool for commanders in the digital battlespace. The system could also be used for immersive augmented reality training to depict unmanned aerial systems and loitering munitions. (US Army photo)

Recent history proves that UASs, used in the right conditions, are deadly and can be decisive. Leaders, both friendly and threat, who recognize this are actively pursuing ways to use UASs and CUASs in the next conflict. Most importantly, the most focused leaders are also looking for ways to train their forces to win in a battlespace saturated with unmanned systems. "The average Soldier, Airman, or Marine lacks adequate counter-UAS training. It's not fully embedded in the [program of instruction] from basic training onward," said Lieutenant-Colonel David Morgan with the Joint Counter-Small Unmanned Aircraft Systems Office's Requirements and Capabilities Division in October 2020. This statement is also accurate for all NATO forces and represents a glaring training deficit. As a result, training for offensive and defensive UAS and CUAS operations in XR has the potential to be the most immediate and cost-effective method to provide immersive training to combat the looming UAS threat.

Tanks have been the main element of offensive mobile striking power for modern armies for over a century. Have unmanned aerial systems, loitering munitions, and artillery and missile long-range precision fires changed this dynamic? In this photo, an Idaho Army National Guard tank fires during training at the Orchard Combat Training Center in Boise, Idaho, May 17, 2021. (US Army photo)

CHAPTER 8

Is the Tank Dead?: The Case for Fifth-Generation Mobile Striking Power

"It must be the role of technology to provide weapons systems which render ineffective costly investment by our foes... by introducing new imponderables into the traditional calculus of battle."

GENERAL DONN A. STARRY, US ARMY (RET,) IN REMARKS DELIVERED AT
A CONFERENCE ON COMBAT VEHICLES, AT FORT KNOX, KY, SEPTEMBER 18, 1986

The proliferation of unmanned aerial systems (UASs), loitering munitions (LMs), long-range precision fires (LRPFs) munitions and networked sensors has created a battlespace dominated by precision fires. The appropriate density and effectiveness of precision fires negates maneuver across this battlespace and forces units and systems to hide and seek cover. The history of warfare shows that whenever fires dominate the battlespace, the battlespace area expands and becomes empty as soldiers and systems go to ground for protection. With no way to mask and limited means to defeat top-attack precision fires, is the tank dead?

Battle cannot be won through precision fires alone without first rendering the enemy's precision fires ineffective, and thus freeing up maneuver, or by maneuver breaking through the enemy's defense and defeating the enemy's precision fire systems as the Azerbaijani's did in the Second Nagorno-Karabakh War. Although there are those who believe that fires alone can win battles and wars, and that the new set of kamikaze LMs and UASs will dominate the battlespace, anything less than annihilation through "massed weapons of precision" merely sets the stage for another round of precision fire strikes and is a one-handed punch, no matter how precise. Precision fires without maneuver will not be decisive. Decision in battle is gained using both fires and maneuver. This two-punch approach has brought decisive outcomes in the past. Fires can set the conditions for success of maneuver, but maneuver across a precision fires saturated battlespace is necessary to generate a decision.

The aim of battle should be the rapid and decisive defeat of the enemy, not the annihilation of every enemy system.

Joint all domain operations are predicated on this premise, that the full spectrum of military force will be used to crack and disintegrate the enemy's domains. The US Army cannot expect to do this with fires alone. To enable maneuver, it must be able to move across the deadly precision fire battlespace to strike at the enemy with sufficient mobile striking power. The battlespace dominated by precision fires can be represented in a simple equation: Seen + Hit = Kill. If it can be seen, it can be hit, and if it can be hit, it can be killed. To break the enemy's domains, this equation must be overturned. We must not be seen. We must limit our signature across the entire electromagnetic spectrum. We must move so rapidly that we cannot be fixed by his fires. We must be able to operate our mobile striking power in the worst-case scenario, under intense cyber-electromagnetic effects. We must have the embedded computing power to operate fifth-generation systems. We must have the computing and networking power to project a false picture of the battlespace to the enemy so that we can maneuver at speed inside a precision fire dominated battlespace with enough striking power to crack his domains and disintegrate his combined arms.

Maneuver can only be restored by rethinking how we design, develop, and employ mobile striking power. The key to winning this deadly scenario will involve the rapid movement of small, self-contained, combined arms armored formations, supported by a wide range of LRPFs, and working hand-in-glove with air and rotary attack forces, to move against the enemy, knock him off balance, and disintegrate his domains and the cohesion of his forces. To maneuver in this battlespace, the US Army needs new equipment developed with a new, multi-domain operations focused, design philosophy. Mobile striking power (MSP) is the ability to conduct sustained direct fire attack and rapid maneuver in a battlespace dominated by precision fires and is a central factor in executing cross-domain maneuver. A next-generation MSP system, a leap-ahead fifth-generation tank, is needed as the central warfighting system to win future high-intensity conflicts. Speed is the priority weapon. The rapid maneuver of MSP must be generated, and human initiative maximized, alongside simplicity, to operate in a degraded environment. MSP is leveraged by precision fires. Precision strikes enable maneuver; maneuver creates shock; shock frustrates enemy decision-making; frustrated enemy decision-making destroys enemy morale; and destroying morale collapses the enemy's will. War is against humans. You can't kill them all. You must make them run. MSP will leverage mission command and maximize decentralized independent action to crack into the enemy's domains and disintegrate his combined arms and anti-air and anti-denial forces.

Effective land power requires the capability to move with speed across the deadly ground, maneuver to the enemy's gaps with formidable striking power, knock him off balance, and place the enemy on the horns of a dilemma where maneuver causes him to either run, surrender, or face destruction. This is the essence of striking power. Striking power, according to World War II German general and panzer prophet Heinz Guderian:

> ... is the power that enables combatants to get close enough to destroy the enemy with their [direct fire] weapons. Only forces that possess this capacity can be reckoned to have true striking power, in other words, have true offensive capacity ... striking power does not consist of firepower alone ... you must bring fire to bear on the enemy by closing the range, identifying the targets that pose the greatest hindrance to the attack, and annihilating them by direct fire.[1]

Striking power is the essential ingredient to "bring the war to a rapid conclusion. All the weapons must cooperate to this end, gauging their own performance and demands according to those of the arms that have the greatest striking power." Striking power generates dominate maneuver. To successfully traverse this deadly battlespace, we still need tanks as a central component of multi-domain operations.

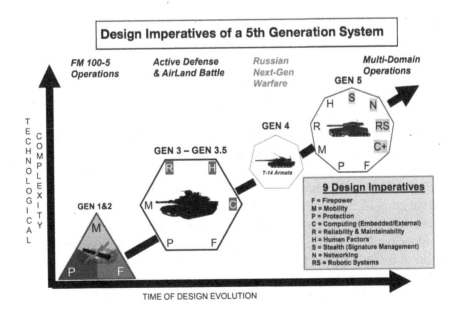

The legacy design philosophy for tank systems is best depicted by a triangle with each side of the triangle representing the specific characteristics of first- to third-generation tanks: mobility, firepower, and protection. With these three characteristics, tanks have enhanced maneuver since WWI.

A pressing question is how to adapt, upgrade or redesign the tank to provide the mobile striking power needed to deter and, if necessary, generate dominant maneuver in a modern, deadlier, battlespace. The answer to the question is to think outside "the triangle." In the past, the primary design factors of the tank were firepower, mobility, and protection. The triangle is no longer sufficient. Today, there is a need for at least nine design parameters: firepower; mobility; protection; computing power (embedded and external); reliability and maintainability; human factors; stealth; networking; and robotic systems.

The "Design Imperatives of a Fifth-Generation System" illustration above depicts the evolution of mobile striking power and why a fifth-generation system is necessary for the US Army to generate dominant maneuver to execute multi-domain operations. The first two generations of tanks represent the traditional requirements of mobility, firepower, and maneuver that were found in the post-World War II main battle tanks (MBT) such as the US M48/M60, the German Leopard 1 and the British Centurion and Chieftain. The third generation includes most of the 120mm-gun armed MBTs such as the American M1A1, the German Leopard 2 and the British Challenger. The third generation included enhanced reliability (better engine maintenance and rapid engine replacement design for example), human factors (separate ammunition storage for example), and computing (better electronic computer systems for targeting, maintenance, and improved situation awareness).

The fourth generation is depicted by the Russian T-14 Armata. Despite the controversy in the West as to the number, capability, and effectiveness of the newly designed Russian T-14, the tank clearly represents a new generation of thinking about mobile striking power. The concept is to have a tank crewed by three soldiers, protected in what is considered the most armored crew compartment ever developed for a vehicle, operating a fully automated turret-gun-system. This "robotic turret" is the future of tank design in that it promises to provide the fusion of accelerated target sensing, identification, and targeting at machine speed. The crew maneuvers the system and then directs the robotic turret to engage. As systems improve, and loading–sensing–identifying–targeting–firing speed is maximized, a robotic turret could revolutionize battlespace target engagements. Imagine if one system, based on the T-14 robotic turret concept, could sense, target, and destroy 12 targets in 60 seconds. The current best rate for the American-built M1A2 SepV3 is roughly 10 rounds a minute. Could a robotic system be built to double that rate of fire and with precision targeting better than what is possible today?

The fifth-generation system that should be built is premised on General Don Starry's concept of rendering ineffective the costly investment by our foes by introducing new imponderables into the traditional calculus of battle. This system must break the precision fires equation that states that what can be sensed and targeted can be hit and killed. Adding the design parameters of stealth, networking, robotic systems, and computing power is imperative to generating maneuver across the precision fires dominated battlespace. The aim of this mobile striking power system is to shatter the enemy's cohesion and will to fight, rather than eroding his forces and materiel through attrition by fires, executed under the decentralized command ethos of mission command.

Precision fires, balanced with dominant maneuver, is the battle-winning solution. This is the warfighting equation the US Army is searching for in its concept of multi-domain operations, where precision fires shape the battlespace, destroy the enemy's anti-air and anti-denial systems, neutralize the opponent's artillery, force the enemy's mobile forces to disperse and go to ground for protection, and then move upon these dispersed enemy forces with great, mobile, striking power. The need today is to rearm and upgrade the force to provide dominant maneuver striking power as the central ingredient of combined arms in an era of precision fires.

Design Parameter	Explanation of Fifth-Generation Capability
Firepower	The enhanced ability to rapidly destroy targets with precision direct fire, especially enemy tanks, anti-tank systems, and infantry (possibly 12 targets/minute or twice the highest rate of fire of the current M1 series tank). This would most likely mean a fully automated turret, with automatic cannon loading system, possibly with more than one cannon per vehicle.
Mobility	The enhanced ability to move across nearly all types of terrain, including most water obstacles, in stride.
Protection	The enhanced ability for passive and active protection of the crew and system from enemy direct fire, indirect fire strikes, and mines. Active protection should include the ability to counter incoming enemy strikes and measures to confuse enemy sensors with decoys and false locations.
Computing power (embedded and external)	The ability to "build the tank around the computer" to provide sufficient computing power to operate all systems in the worst-case scenario (intense electronic warfare and cyber attack).

(Continued)

Design Parameter	Explanation of Fifth-Generation Capability
Reliability and maintainability	The ability to maneuver at the operational depth required to penetrate, crack, and disintegrate the enemy's A2/AD and Precision Fires domain without conducting intensive refueling operations and the ability to maintain the vehicle's systems throughout this effort.
Human factors	The enhanced ability to protect the human crew, most likely by placing them in the hull.
Stealth	The enhanced ability to approach invisibility across the electromagnetic spectrum.
Networking	The enhanced ability to electronically network with all friendly systems to provide situation awareness, in the worst-case scenarios under intense electronic warfare and cyber attack.
Robotic systems	The enhanced ability to work with robotic wingman systems that are commanded, not controlled, by the human-operated mobile striking power platform. This ability to command, not control the robotic systems, must operate under the worst-case scenario so soldiers remain fighters, not controllers. The robot systems follow the human commanders' lead and obey simplified "battle drill" commands. Robots reinforce by thickening the battlefield with additional combat power.

The tempo and lethality of war is accelerating. Smarter, more precise weapons, linked to ubiquitous sensors, have created a very deadly battlespace. The recent Azerbaijan–Armenian war demonstrated this point and exposed the weakness of traditional thinking concerning how to fight modern wars. With the dramatic success of precision unmanned aerial weapons against armored vehicles in this war, many question the role of the MBT. Tanks still play a critical role in war, but they must become more agile to survive and win in this new, more lethal battlespace. Nearly every MBT in the world today was developed during the Cold War and as they are upgraded with additional armor, larger caliber cannons, and active and passive protection systems, they are getting heavier and agility is suffering. The agility of a tank is its ability to accelerate, turn, jink, and stop. To move heavier MBTs, powerful engines that generate tremendous horsepower are required. You also need a reliable transmission that can reduce and vary the higher engine speed to the slower speed of the tank track. Thus, the engine and the transmission are the critical components of agility. In his *Tank Warfare*, the late, great, tank expert, Richard Simpkin, stated that the most important factor in tank agility is the tank's power-weight ratio, the horsepower (hp) available per ton of tank weight.

A comparison of the Russian T-90M and the Republic of Korea's K2 Black Panther reveals the current state of the technology.

The T-90M Proryv-3 (Breakthrough) tank is a state of the art, third-generation MBT and provides the Russian Army with a powerful and survivable tank with better protection, firepower and increased mobility than other tanks in the inventory. The T-90M is the most important tank in the Russian arsenal as it merges the best design aspects of the T-72 and T-80. Developed by the Russian defense company UralVagonZavod (UVZ), the largest main battle tank manufacturer in the world, it is an upgrade of the Proryv-2. The tank incorporates a new turret, the cannon developed for the T-14 Armata, a new engine, and costs approximately US$4.5 million. These upgrades increased the tank's weight from 46 tons to 50 tons, requiring a more powerful engine to maintain agility. The T-90M's new powerplant is the V-96, 12-cylinder diesel engine which produces 1,250–1,300 hp, generating 26hp per ton when mated with a new, Russian-developed automatic transmission. This is the most powerful engine and transmission of any Russian tank and UVZ developed this combination based on previously proven designs.

The Republic of Korea (ROK) has fielded a new tank, the K2 Black Panther MBT. It is regarded as the most advanced and expensive tank in the world. Developed by Hyundai Rotem, an affiliate of the Hyundai Motor Group, each K2 tank costs US$8.5 million dollars and has cutting edge features including the ability to fire the KSTAM (Korea Smart Top Attack Munition) from its 120mm cannon. Introduced in 2009, the K2 started with the dependable German-designed MTU MT-883 Ka-501 4-cycle, 12-cylinder water-cooled diesel engine from the Tognum Group, one of the largest global suppliers of diesel engines, coupled with a German-designed RENK transmission. Hyundai Rotem subsequently developed its own tank engine and transmission for the K2. The latest version uses a South Korean-made Doosan DV27K 4-cycle, 12-cylinder water-cooled diesel and a South Korean-made S&T Dynamics automatic transmission. The DV27K generates 1,500hp and provides a power to weight ratio of 27.3hp per ton. The fully automatic transmission of the vehicle includes five forward and three reverse gears. Problems with the new transmission in late 2020 caused the South Koreans to replace it with the reliable RENK unit. In addition, the ROK has negotiated a deal with Turkey to export the K2's technologies, but the problems with the S&T Dynamics transmission have delayed Turkey's new Altay MBT development plans. The problem with the transmission illustrates how difficult it is to design an effective and reliable engine and transmission combination to move heavy MBTs.

In 2019, Germany and France agreed to work together on a future ground combat system called the Main Ground Combat System (MGCS). Rheinmetall, one of Europe's leading suppliers of armored vehicles (such as the Leopard MBT, MBT advanced technology demonstrator, Lynx infantry fighting vehicle, Kodiak armored engineer vehicle, and the Wiesel light reconnaissance vehicle), has developed a forward-thinking tank design for the MGCS. The French–German Research Institute of Saint-Louis (ISL) is coordinating the design and development of the MGCS. This process involves the design of a family of vehicles that will have different capabilities, both manned and unmanned, to complement each other and operate together as a team. Development plans call for five phases: operational requirements analysis, concepts study, technology development and demonstration, system integration and demonstration, and system production. Initial reports describe one design as a two-man tank with an unmanned turret. The two human operators are seated in the hull in a specially armored, protected "survival-cell" capsule. By reducing the number of crew members, and protecting them in a smaller area, the MGCS needs less armor. Since the common factor for tank design is roughly 10 tons of armored weight per crew member, the Rheinmetall design could significantly reduce the vehicle's weight. The design has the engine in the hull's front and the chassis will borrow its configuration from the KF41 Lynx. The main armament could be a conventional cannon or possibly an electro-thermal-chemical gun. The tank's controls will be digital. This new design will require an abundance of electrical power, so the engine could be a hybrid or all-electric with an electric cross drive transmission. The ISL has completed both the operational requirements analysis and the concept study and is currently in the technology development phase. The MGCS is an ambitious program scheduled for production in 2035.

	T-90M	K2 Black Panther	MGCS
Engine Type	V-96 12-cylinder diesel engine	DV27K 4-cycle, 12-cylinder water-cooled diesel engine	Hybrid or All Electric?
Engine Horsepower	930kW/1,300hp	1118.5kW/1,500hp	TBD
Tank Weight	50 tons	55 tons	30 tons or less?
Power to Weight Ratio	26hp per ton / 19.38kW per ton	27.3hp per ton / 20.35kW per ton	TBD
Road Speed	65km/hr	70km/hr	TBD

Military procurement is a ponderous and difficult process in the best of situations and hinders the design and fielding of totally new systems to replace legacy platforms. Sticking with what works, and incrementally improving current equipment is usually a safer bet, until it no longer is. Today, the 1,500hp power-rating has become the standard for modern MBT with even the Russians moving to upgrade their latest engines from 1,300hp. The current generation of MBT engines and transmissions have improved as much as current technology will allow. It requires new thinking to change this equation. New hybrid and electric designs are on the horizon and promise significant advantages over conventional turbine and diesel engines. Hybrid electric drives are smaller than conventional diesel engines, require a simpler drive train, have 40 percent fewer moving parts compared to diesel engines, and promise to provide 20 percent better fuel efficiency. They also produce ample electricity for modern tank computer and onboard C4ISR (Command, Control, Communications, Computers, Intelligence, Surveillance and Reconnaissance) systems. Today, no hybrid or electric engines are used on MBTs. As new engine technologies improve, however, future MBTs must move in this direction. Until combat vehicle designers start thinking differently, the diesel engine, with about 1,500 hp and a reliable transmission, will rule.

Elbit's Systems See-Through Armor has been in the works for five or more years and represents a cost-effective means to enhance existing armored vehicles. (elbitsystems.com/Elbitmain/files/See-Through_Armor.pdf)

See-through armor

Killer tank commanders—that special breed of armored fighting vehicle commander who always got off the first shot, always hit the target and seemed to have a sixth sense on the battlefield—learned to fight with their heads and shoulders exposed outside the turret. They had to do this to survive and win. Tank commanders needed to see in order to gain situational awareness (SA). Armored vehicles are deadly, noisy and require the full focus of the vehicle commander. Pilots of high-performance aircraft experience the same challenge. Protecting the pilot has always been a priority in the design of military aircraft, but the top priority for the most successful aircraft designs has been to create better pilot SA. Canopies are usually made of the best bullet-resistant transparent materials, but the pilot, like his tank commander counterpart, operates exposed to enemy fire.

Today, modern combat aircraft have sophisticated heads-up displays to overlay critical information and provide early warning of threats, but pilots still need to "see-through" the cockpit to fly. The need for a transparent cockpit is waning, however, as new technology is allowing the pilot to see through the skin of the aircraft and gain unprecedented SA. Lockheed Martin has developed this capability for its most technologically advanced multi-role fighter, the F-35 Lightning II. "As F-35 pilots," said Lockheed Martin F-35 test pilot Billie Flynn, "we see imagery collected from six different cameras embedded all around the aircraft, fed into one seamless picture of landscape projected in the glass of our helmet. This allows us to quite literally look all around and effectively 'see-through' the skin of the airplane – as if the jet structure is not even there." Advanced aircraft systems like these are now being adapted to land systems and promise to become the future of manned armored fighting vehicle SA.

Israel has been a leader in tank and armored fighting vehicle systems for decades and the Israeli Armored Corps took pride in the fact its tank commanders fought with their head and shoulders outside of the tank, saw the enemy first, fired first and hit. Increased tank commander casualties in close-quarters city fighting, however, has compelled the IDF to seek new ways to protect them while still providing the SA needed to win the tactical fight. With the increased miniaturization and sophistication of high-definition cameras and networked sensors, Elbit created a See-Through Armor (STA) system that can be added to existing armored vehicles. The key features of STA include a continuous and seamless 360-degree panoramic view, with the entire crew fully protected under armor; advanced image processing to provide enhanced battle information; day and night vision with zoom capability; and the ability to integrate STA into Elbit's Closed Hatches concept that integrates remote control weapon stations and a battle management system.[2] STA is primarily a screen-based system that could be enhanced by adding a head-mounted display, possibly even with a commercial off-the-shelf system such as Facebook's Oculus Rift virtual reality headset or the Daqri Smart Helmet, an augmented reality headset. These headsets would allow the vehicle commander to achieve enhanced SA while allowing his/her hands to be free to activate weapons or vehicle controls.

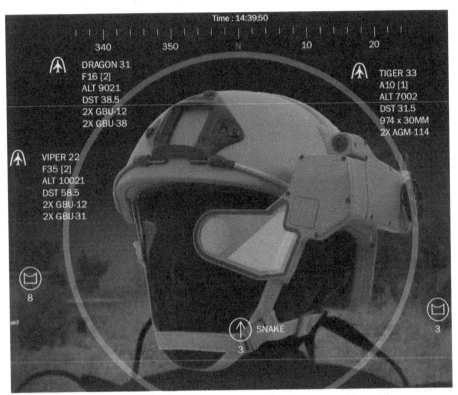

BAE Systems, a British multinational arms, security, and aerospace company based in London, England, is adapting its revolutionary Q-Warrior helmet-mounted display for armored vehicles. With proper software and multi-domain sensor input, soldiers equipped with this helmet could be warned of threats from unmanned aerial systems, loitering mentions, and long-range precision fires from artillery and missiles in time to take protective measures. (BAE image)

Battleview 360

The Battleview 360 system is the most sophisticated transformation of an aircraft-like SA system for armored fighting vehicles. Networking a set of cameras and sensors onto an armored vehicle, and using the advances provided by the BAE-developed Q-Warrior helmet-mounted display (HMD), BAE demonstrated their version of an STA system in the second half of 2015. Developed by BAE's Swedish subsidiary Hägglunds, Battleview 360 combines networked cameras, sensors and an HMD with 3D digital mapping technology to create an accurate view and an enhanced 3D map of the vehicle's battlespace. The HMD can be linked to visual and infrared cameras on the outside of the vehicle to "see-through" the armor in daylight and during limited visibility. In addition, any troops sitting in a troop compartment of an armored vehicle can access the system with an HMD or tablet to gain SA while inside the vehicle.

The ability to enhance the SA of an armored vehicle crew, while keeping the crew under the protection of armor, seems to have been realized by Elbit and BAE in their recent developments in STA technology. The key question to ask, however, is if this is solving the right problem? Rather than enhancing the SA of the crew and their survivability, why not develop a way to replace the crew entirely? The best STA of the next decade may be found in unmanned armored vehicle systems where the tank is operated from far away, by a human in sanctuary, as unmanned aerial vehicles are flown today.

It is high hubris to believe all things are different in our modern times. The tank is not dead and the UAS is not a "silver bullet" solution to win all future wars. The design of tanks must change if we expect to maximize their role to provide mobile striking power. Tactics, techniques and procedures must change as well. Hard training and the execution of many combat simulations can help show the way forward. The hard lessons of past wars still provide us with the opportunity to learn and extrapolate strategies for future wars. In 1940, the French opted for a technologically superior firepower solution to win battle and war. They failed when their "fires domain" was cracked and disintegrated by the maneuver of mobile striking power. We cannot rely on a technological Maginot Line. The argument that we will simply apply precision fires and destroy the majority, if not all, of the enemy's forces, and therefore break their will, is historically incorrect. It did not work in 1940 and anything less than a "precision weapon of mass destruction" will not work today. Deterring war will require mobile striking power to generate dominant maneuver in an era of precision fires. To have dominant maneuver, you need a dominant tank. When maneuver and fires work in tandem, the possibilities of decisive battlespace results increase. We must be able to maneuver across a precision fires dominated battlespace. Technology currently under development can provide many of the answers to break the precision firepower equation. We must develop a design philosophy that will enable us to develop a fifth-generation mobile striking power system that can bring maneuver to the new battlespace.

The Future of the Tank

"The battlespace is now transparent. Advanced sensor networks can observe with an unblinking eye. Long-range precision fires and a host of unmanned systems will impede maneuver. In this high-tech arena, we will need tanks to deliver maneuver, firepower and shock effect, but the tank must transform. We must build new tanks that can mask from enemy sensors. We must develop new tactics, techniques, and procedures to operate with greater dispersion. The future tank is a multi-domain, mobile, protected, firepower node that automatically meshes with an array of flying drones and ground robotic systems to return ground maneuver to the battlespace."

John Antal, lecture on the Second Nagorno-Karabakh War at the US Army Fires in MultiDomain Transformation Conference at Fort Sill, Oklahoma, September 2, 2021

Camouflage, the art of not being seen, is vital to survive in today's battlespace, but traditional camouflage proved ineffective in hiding Armenian forces from Azerbaijani sensors, loitering munitions, and unmanned aerial systems during the Second Nagorno-Karabakh War. In this photo, an M1A2 Abrams tank, camouflaged in the traditional fashion, emerges out of wooded terrain. Soldiers assigned to the 4th Infantry Division's 1st Battalion, 68th Armor Regiment, 3rd Armored Brigade Combat Team, had concealed it to blend in with the surrounding environment at Presidential Range in Swietozow, Poland, on January 20, 2017. Traditional camouflage will not fool modern sensors and new methods of masking are required to survive and maneuver in the modern battlespace. (US Army photo, Staff Sergeant Elizabeth Tarr)

CHAPTER 9

Masking: Why masking is a priority in the modern battlespace

"In the modern battlespace, the emergence of precision-guided munitions requires militaries to conceal their forces because, in order to conduct these operations (combined arms) successfully, usually you need to be able to mass your forces to achieve a breakthrough on the frontline."

FRANZ-STEFAN GADY, RESEARCH FELLOW
AT THE INTERNATIONAL INSTITUTE FOR STRATEGIC STUDIES[1]

All warfare is based on deception. Becoming invisible to the enemy is the ultimate form of deception. The struggle between finding and hiding is as old as war itself. In the past, those who could camouflage themselves, by blending into their surroundings, gained the advantage of making it difficult for their forces to be targeted and in launching attacks with surprise. During World War II, the Royal Navy struggled to counter specially designed magnetic "influence" naval mines. Earlier naval mines were contact detonated. The ship had to hit the mine with enough force to set off the detonators to explode the mine. Anyone who has ever watched a World War II submarine movie has seen these mines: weapons that resemble metal balls with spikes suspended by iron chains. These mines were placed at a depth a ship would strike them. The Germans decided to create a new type of mine, one that didn't require direct contact with an approaching ship. This mine had a sensor that could detect a passing ship's magnetic field. Because of the principle of ferromagnetism, every steel ship generates a magnetic signature. Invisible to the naked eye, this magnetic field is strong enough to be identified by specially designed sensors.

The Germans put their best scientists to work to develop an underwater mine that could be launched by ship, boat, or aircraft that would detonate when the mechanism in the mine recognized a difference in the local magnetic field. The Germans measured the ship's magnetic field by a unit they termed a "gauss." Once a German magnetic mine detected the proper electromagnetic field was passing nearby, and the ship registered the appropriate level of gauss, the mine detonated, sending a shockwave toward the nearby ship. The shockwave was powerful enough to at least severely damage any ship or submarine in the Royal Navy. The typical German magnetic influence mine held 300 kilograms (660lb) of explosive. This magnetic "influence" mine, designated as the Mark I Magnetic Mine by the Germans, was a carefully guarded secret and was deployed with success in 1939. The British captured two mines dropped from German aircraft that landed in the mud bank of the Thames Estuary. From this, they developed methods to clear magnetic influence mines, but it was a slow and dangerous process. Then, just before the German blitzkrieg burst across the borders of Belgium, Luxembourg and France in May 1940, the British came up with the concept of degaussing and deperming.

Degaussing involved adding special electromagnetic coils to the ships that was time-consuming and expensive, especially since it involved coils of copper wire and copper was in high demand and short supply to the British in 1940. Deperming, also called "wiping," involved dragging electrical cable, that emitted a 2000 amperes electrical charge, along the side of the ship to demagnetize the hull. This procedure masked the ship's hull to magnetic

Masking is vital for submarines. Deperming or degaussing are procedures for masking a vessel's magnetic signature from magnetic detection vessels and mines. In this photo, the USS *Jimmy Carter* (SSN-23) is degaussed at the US Naval Base at Kitsap Peninsula in Washington state. (US Navy photo).

influence mines for up to six months. After that, the process needed to be repeated to ensure demagnetization.

As German tanks bottled up the British Expeditionary Force at Dunkirk, German bombers dropped hundreds of magnetic influence mines to stop any naval evacuation. The noose was tightening and it looked as if the British and French soldiers on the beach would have to fight to the death or surrender. The chief of the German air force, Generalfeldmarschall Hermann Göring, ensured Adolf Hitler that his *Luftwaffe* would destroy any Royal Navy ships that attempted to rescue the 380,000-plus troops stranded on the beaches of Dunkirk, either by direct action or the thousands of magnetic influence mines his bombers had sown in the English Channel. Little did Göring know that the British realized the threat in time. Reacting to the challenge with dogged determination, the British used the new deperming system to demagnetize 400 ships in four days. Those ships became invisible to the German magnetic mines. This helped to make the "Miracle of Dunkirk" possible, and the beleaguered British were able to evacuate 340,000 troops to England.

Today's battlespace

In modern air warfare, to tip the balance in favor of the offense and counter the unblinking eye of new radar systems, stealth aircraft were developed. Stealth aircraft use combinations of sophisticated low observable technologies to minimize the radar signature of an aircraft, masking the radar, infrared, visible light, radio frequency spectrum, and audio signature. An F-22 Raptor, for instance, appears as small as a bumble bee on some radar scopes. Stealth aircraft are not invisible, but their stealth technology makes them difficult to target.

A similar tug-of-war is happening in land warfare. The convergence of long-range precision fires (LRPFs), sensor networks, and artificial intelligence (AI) threatens to dominate the battlespace of the next war. A combination of satellites, unmanned aerial vehicles (UAVs), and micro-electro-mechanical systems (MEMS) technology has enabled sensor networks that can identify and track targets across the electromagnetic spectrum (EMS). AI-enabled automated targeting and fire control is being perfected to engage ground targets. Smart, super-fast, extremely lethal, interconnected LRPF weapons, and extended range artillery systems using cluster bomb munitions, presage the delivery of a level of lethality and accuracy never seen on the battlespace. This disruption threatens to make the traditional concept of combined arms maneuver impossible.

To achieve this level of tactical overmatch will require ample quantities of artillery and rocket firepower. The Russian Army is often described as an "Artillery Army with lots of tanks." With the convergence of LRPF, sensor networks, and AI, the Russian vision of an automated, reconnaissance, strike complex will be realized before 2040. According to the Deputy Chief of Staff of Ground Forces, Major General Vadim Marusin, "Today, the cycle (reconnaissance–engagement) takes literally 10 seconds."[2] In short, the Russians intend to rule the battlespace with artillery and rocket firepower.

The traditional method to defeat an enemy's long-range firepower capability is to employ counter long-range firepower, knocking out the enemy's fire units, and gaining and maintaining fire superiority. The best military minds of World War I tried this method with catastrophic and unsuccessful results.

Masking is the full-spectrum, multi-domain effort to deceive enemy sensors and disrupt enemy targeting. It is the active and passive ability to make military systems difficult or impossible to identify, locate, and target. For the past 60 years, US and NATO forces have reduced their dependency on rockets and artillery by leveraging airpower to gain fire superiority. With the Russians deploying arguably the best air defense systems in the world, including the S-400 "Triumph," S-500 "Prometheus," and the new Alabuga electro-magnetic pulse (EMP) missile program, they can challenge, and possibly negate, the US and NATO airpower advantage, especially in the early stages of a conflict. China has similar capabilities. Since the air domain is now contested by potential adversaries—as are the other domains of land, sea, space and cyber—the ability to gain fire superiority over the battle area is now in doubt.

This reconnaissance strike and conventional artillery capability presents a terrifying equation: everything on the battlespace will be sensed, targeted, and rapidly destroyed by LRPFs, or massed, conventional artillery firing cluster bombs with great accuracy. Furthermore, in any future conflict with Russia or China, the side that strikes first has a marked advantage. If future war can be considered analogous to a five-dimensional chess game, then the Russians and Chinese are playing the "white" pieces and thus have the first move. In such a case, the survival of troops and vehicles in the extended battle area, which has expanded to depths around 500 kilometers (310 miles) or greater, will be in jeopardy. Unless forces can rapidly dig in deep enough to protect themselves from this intense firepower, they must find a way to hide.

Soldiers and systems require a means to mask from enemy sensors and targeting. Masking is more than camouflage and stealth. It employs next-generation active and passive means to reduce the EMS signature to render the system difficult to locate and hard to target. Some of these technologies could include:

Masking

Masking is the full-spectrum, multi-domain effort to deceive enemy sensors and disrupt enemy targeting.

- Advanced profile and vehicle design to lower a vehicle's radar cross-section and reduce its thermal, electronic, and acoustic signature.
- Low-tech, passive systems such as next-generation multispectral camouflage netting, which conceals objects from detection across several portions of the electromagnetic spectrum at the same time.[3]
- Color-changing materials and radar-absorbing paint.
- Intelligent, multispectral camouflage systems to rapidly blend a vehicle into its surrounding EMS background.
- Multispectral smoke intended to mask ground military equipment from top-attack by precision weapons by creating a curtain of aerosol interference that deceives the enemy's high-precision ammunition guidance systems.[4]
- Decoys and portrayal of false actions and locations in multiple domains.
- Cognitive electronic warfare systems employing machine-learning to counter the enemy's radars.
- Electronic jamming to protect the emissions of friendly communications and electronic systems against enemy detection.
- Cyber and electronic warfare support measures and signals intelligence to barrage enemy sensors with false readings and "false positives" making the sensors see many more targets than are there.
- The use of electronic countermeasures and digital radio frequency memory to hide beneath the blanket of enemy or friendly jamming.
- The use of tactical EMP weapons that would affect systems inside the strike zone by "blinding" or overloading to the main electronic elements and systems.[5]

Masking is a logical necessity and should become a priority for land power systems development, just as stealth became essential for the survival of our air power platforms. In the ageless competition between hiders and finders, the finders are winning. In the modern battlespace, all forces require the ability to hide in order to survive. What can be seen by sensors, that can now locate emissions across the electromagnetic spectrum, will be killed. Masking includes, but is not limited to, technologies that enable spectrum management and the low probability of detection in the electromagnetic, acoustic, seismic and thermal spectrums; intelligent, multispectral camouflage systems; decoys and spoofs; cognitive electronic warfare systems employing machine learning to counter the enemy's radars; and the use of jamming, electronic countermeasures and digital radio frequency memory to hide and operate beneath the blanket of enemy or friendly jamming.

The intention of masking is not invisibility, which may be possible, but the ability to reduce the probability of detection, confuse the enemy's targeting system with false readings, and make them shoot at ghosts that they cannot

The OBRUM PL-01 is a Polish tank that will use ADAPTIV active camouflage designed by BAE Systems. According to the BAE website, ADAPTIV was developed and patented in Sweden after the Swedish Defense Materiel Administration commissioned BAE Systems in Örnsköldsvik to produce full-scale technology for land vehicles to avoid detection from thermal sensor systems. After three years of challenging research, a project team of seven people, with expertise in the fields of problem solving, software, sensors, electronics and design, developed this unique solution. This masking solution could make a tank appear as a landscape, a helicopter as a cloud, or a warship as a wave. "The high-tech pixels that make up the ADAPTIV system can also be resized to achieve stealth at different ranges. For example, larger objects like buildings or warships might not require close-up stealth and may be fitted with larger panels to display a lower resolution image." The US Army has not pursued the use of the sophisticated ADAPTIV active camouflage technology for its vehicle fleet. (Polish Ministry of National Defense photo)

accurately locate. Sun Tzu, the ancient sage of war, understood masking when he stated the most refined form you can give your troops is to make them "as hard to know as shadows." The ability to mask ground systems, and turn them into shadows, would be a revolutionary shift in survival in a future battlespace.

21st-century camouflage

Camouflage is the art of concealment and the ability to become invisible is an advantage that is being pursued by many nations. Ground military units use radar and laser scattering camouflage nets to inhibit detection from ground and air sensors. Hiding objects in the spectrum visible to the human eye can be handled by conventional camouflage techniques, but cloaking an object from radio, radar and heat wavelengths is the key to military invisibility. In the next 10–15 years, technological advances promise to provide military units with more active means to hide from the enemy. Research into active camouflage systems and invisibility is accelerating with the potential to change how wars are fought.

For centuries, camouflage has been about adapting to your surroundings and blending in with the terrain and vegetation. In nature, through natural selection, those animals that could change their color to hide in their habitats increased their ability to survive. The chameleon, for example, will change colors to match its background. Similarly, the squid has a unique, natural ability that has made it an expert at hiding from its enemies. Learning from the squid, a team of researchers from the UK's Engineering and Mathematics Department at the University of Bristol have developed a breakthrough in camouflage. Their latest research into the development of artificial cephalopod chromophores—the cells that allow squids to change color—is laying the foundation for smart materials that will instantly change color to match their surroundings. This research was released in 2015 and published in a paper titled: "Hiding the Squid: Patterns in Artificial Cephalopod Skin," by Aaron Fishman, Jonathan Rossiter, and Martin Homer. The paper postulates "an application of smart materials, inspired by biological chromophores, to generate active dynamic patterns ... and concludes with a discussion of the potential of our system for future pattern generation in artificial skin."

In 2018, the University of California at Irving (UCI) created a smart material that will render objects invisible to infrared light and thermal night vision devices. Engineers Alon Gorodetsky and Chengyi Xu of UCI published their paper, "Adaptive Infrared Reflecting Systems Inspired by Cephalopods," in the magazine *Science* on March 30, 2018. Gorodetsky and

Xu proposed that their study can "open opportunities for infrared camouflage and other technologies that regulate infrared radiation." Gorodetsky also reported:

> We've developed stickers for use as a thin, flexible layer of camo with the potential to take on a pattern that will better match the soldiers' infrared reflectance to their background and hide them from active infrared visualization ... We're going after something that's inexpensive and completely disposable. You take out this protein-coated tape, you use it quickly to make an appropriate camouflage pattern on the fly, then you take it off and throw it away.[6]

Adaptive camouflage

Vehicles need a different means of camouflage and researchers are developing adaptive camouflage to cloak vehicles. Adaptive camouflage uses optical technology to replace the image of what is masked with an image of the background. This can be accomplished by placing a thin screen between the observer and the concealed object and generating the image of the background in real-time. BAE Systems has developed this concept into a prototype, state of the art, technology system called ADAPTIV for armored vehicles. ADAPTIV generates real-time active camouflaging of military vehicles. BAE reports its technology works by:

> ... using lightweight hexagonal pixels which are electrically powered by the vehicle's systems. The pixels are individually heated and cooled using commercially available semi-conducting technology. The hand-sized pixels are made of metal, so that they can sustain physical impact and provide defense against enemy ordnance. The entire system has been designed with ease of use in mind, and the pixels are able to be easily and rapidly removed and replaced if damaged. Once mounted on a vehicle's hull or ballistic armor plates, ADAPTIV renders a vehicle invisible to infra-red and other surveillance technology. Whether it is day or night, whether they are on the move or stationary, ADAPTIV provides vehicles increased stealth and greater survivability. ADAPTIV allows the vehicle to blend into the natural surroundings and significantly reduces detection.[7]

In demonstrations of the ADAPTIV system conducted in 2011, a tank with BAE's camouflage appeared as a civilian automobile in thermal and infrared imaging devices. The ADAPTIV active electronic-camouflage system also includes an identification, friend or foe system that will differentiate allies from enemies. Poland's OBRUM has been collaborating with BAE Systems on designing a main battle tank, the PL-01, which employs ADAPTIV active camouflage. BAE says ADAPTIV can be used for ground vehicles, ships, and installations and reports it is the latest breakthrough in stealth technology.

Active cloaking

An object is observed when the electromagnetic waves scattered from that object are detected by the human eye or some other sensor. A device that can "correct" or cancel that scattering would hide the object. In 2013, George V. Eleftheriades of the University of Toronto reported that "to make our approach work for visible light, is to surround the object with optical antennas and control what they radiate—color, amplitude and delay—precisely." Active cloaking, therefore, would surround the object to be cloaked with electromagnetic sources specifically designed to cancel the electromagnetic field scattered by the object. In November 2017, researchers at Beersheba's Ben-Gurion University of the Negev in Israel created a "cloaking chip" that scatters and bends light around the object so that the light does not interact with the object. The Israeli study, titled "Invisibility: Cloaking Scheme by Evanescent Fields Distortion on Composite Plasmonic Waveguides with Si Nano-Spacer," by Yakov Galutin, Eran Falek and Alina Karabchevsk, claimed the chip could be used to enhance radar-absorbing paint for stealth aircraft.

ADAPTIV technology applied to a HPK15B helicopter. ADAPTIV was developed by BAE Systems as an active camouflage system to generate infrared stealth for military vehicles. It is designed to make detection by far infrared night vision devices difficult and consists of an array of hexagonal Peltier plates which, when heated and cooled, form any desired image, such as the natural background or of a non-target object. The purpose of the ADAPTIV technology project is to develop stealth ground vehicles. (BAE Systems photo)

Metamaterials

The limitation of ADAPTIV and other cloaking systems is thickness and bulk. The normal condition of shining a light on an object is reflection and absorption. What if you could create a material that did not reflect or absorb light? In 2006, physicist Professor Sir John Pendry from Imperial College London announced it should be possible to bend light to create invisibility. Pendry pioneered the concept of designing metamaterials—materials that have optical properties not found in nature—to develop an "invisibility cloak." He received the Newton Medal, the highest honor of the UK's Physics Institute, for his "seminal contributions to surface science, disordered systems and photonics" (the theoretical foundation of generating invisibility). Building upon the concept of bending light waves, researchers at the University of California, San Diego, recently created a new metamaterial from ultra-thin Teflon substrate that, when combined with ceramic cylinders, renders objects invisible to incoming waves. This metamaterial enables electromagnetic radiation to pass freely around the object. A study by LiYi Hsu, Thomas Lepetit, and Boubacar Kanté, titled "Extremely Thin Dielectric Metasurface for Carpet Cloaking," proposed that "carpet cloaking with an extremely thin dielectric metasurface is possible." According to Kanté, this approach provides for a cloaking system that is both thin and does not alter the brightness of light around a hidden object. Many cloaks are glossy because they are made with metal particles which absorb light. The researchers report that one of the keys to their cloak's design is the use of non-conductive materials called dielectrics which, unlike metals, do not absorb light. This cloak includes two dielectrics, a proprietary ceramic and Teflon, which are structurally tailored on a very fine scale to change the way light waves reflect off the cloak. Such a metamaterial could render many military systems nearly invisible to most means of detection and would have an immediate application in enhancing the stealth capabilities of aircraft and unmanned aerial vehicles (UAVs).

True invisibility, the ultimate camouflage, is a property that exists at the atomic level. In January 2018, researchers at the Northwestern University of Evanston, Illinois, published their findings in the online journal *Science*, offering another way to manipulate light to achieve invisibility. Their study, "Building Superlattices from Individual Nanoparticles via Template-confined DNA mediated Assembly" reveals a breakthrough in developing metamaterials that combined DNA assembly with gold nanoparticles to produce stimuli-responsive metamaterials. This new method precisely arranges nanoparticles of different shapes and sizes and shapes in two and three dimensions, resulting in optically active superlattices. These can be programmed to change into any visible color. Professors Chad Mirkin, Vinayak Dravid and Koray Aydin used a process known as "DNA assembly" and "top-down lithography" to organize nanoparticles in two and three dimensions. "So now we have a type of architectural control where we can build crystalline-type lattices with all the defined parameters that we want," reported Mirkin, Director of the International Institute for Nanotechnology at Northwestern. The Institute is a global hub that currently represents and integrates more than US$600 million in cutting-edge nanotechnology research and is one of the largest nanotechnology research centers in the world. "We can make structures that nobody has ever even conceived of before; this is a true man-over-nature event."

The Chinese have also been hard at work to crack the secret of invisibility. Researchers at the State Key Laboratory of Millimeter Waves at Southeast University in Nanjing, Jiangsu province, China's leading institute on the research of thin-membrane metamaterials for defense applications, publicly announced in March 2018 they had developed a breakthrough metamaterial that would cloak military aircraft from radar, making them stealth-like. Liu Ruopeng, the president of the Kuang-Chi Aircraft Company, who used to work at the Nanjing University laboratory, told the Chinese news website *Ifeng.com* that China was well ahead of other countries in applying metamaterials to aircraft. If this is true, then the Chinese military may adapt these new metamaterials to a wide range of aircraft and UAVs.

The theory of using metamaterials to create invisibility has now been mathematically proven. Scientists from around the globe are making key breakthroughs in new ways to develop metamaterials from exotic composites of metal, ceramic, Teflon and fiber. These metamaterials are described best by author and physicist Michio Kaku in his book *Physics of the Impossible*:

> Think about the way a river flows around a boulder. Because the water quickly wraps around the bolder, the presence of the boulder has been washed out downstream. Similarly, metamaterials can continuously alter and bend the path of microwaves so that they flow around a cylinder, for example, essentially making everything inside the cylinder invisible to microwaves. If the metamaterial can eliminate all reflection and shadows, then it can render an object totally invisible to that form of radiation … At the heart of metamaterials is the ability to manipulate something called the "index of refraction." Refraction is the bending of light as it moves through a transparent media… If one could control the index of refraction inside a metamaterial so that light passed around the object, then the object would become invisible.[8]

The ability of science to manipulate this index of refraction is accelerating and metamaterials that can manipulate light in unconventional ways have been produced. Harnessing metamaterials to block, enhance and absorb light is the next step in developing brilliant camouflage that will provide a powerful military advantage in the years to come.

Is masking possible in an increasingly transparent battlespace? Stealth was initially considered impossible for aircraft, until breakthroughs in multiple fields occurred and suddenly stealth aircraft were possible. Military leaders and technology developers should think carefully about the character of the future battlespace and then take steps to address what is needed to survive and win on that battlespace. As Sun Tzu said, all warfare is based on deception. In an increasingly lethal and transparent battlespace, being able to mask and become difficult to target is a prerequisite, not just a priority.

Masking

"Masking is the full-spectrum, multi-domain effort to deceive enemy
sensors and disrupt enemy targeting.
In the modern battlespace, you either mask or die."

John Antal, lecture on the Second Nagorno-Karabakh War at the US
Army Fires in MultiDomain Transformation Conference at Fort Sill,
Oklahoma, September 2, 2021

Masking requires a full-spectrum solution of active and passive measures to make systems and personnel difficult or impossible to target. The thermal camouflage system is made by the Israeli company Fibrotex. This thermal covering reduces the thermal signature of the tank, making it difficult for enemy sensors to observe and for unmanned combat aerial vehicles, loitering munitions and long-range precision fires to target. The material does not restrict the tank's mobility and it can be placed on the tank for mobile operations. (Fibrotex image)

CHAPTER 10

War at the Speed of Thought

"Winning time is winning battle."
V. G. REZNICHENKO, IN *TAKTIKA*, 1984[1]

The race belongs to the swift; thus there is a contest today to leverage artificial intelligence (AI) to increase the speed of execution, accuracy, and lethality of military systems. There are three general categories of AI: artificial narrow intelligence (ANI), artificial general intelligence (AGI), and artificial super intelligence (ASI). ANI surrounds us today and is the application of algorithms that enable machines to complete specific, narrow tasks to solve problems. AGI is the next level of AI and is the hypothetical ability of a computer to think at the level of a human being and master any intellectual task a human can learn. AGI is the goal of many AI developers and nations, but no true AGI has yet been created. Most researchers believe it will be several decades, at best, before the birth of true AGI. When it is perfected, the possibility has been theorized that, if left to itself, several AGIs in communication with each other could exponentially evolve into ASI, surpassing the cognitive abilities of humans. AGI and ASI is what Elon Musk, the founder, CEO, chief technology engineer and chief designer of SpaceX; early investor, CEO and product architect of Tesla; founder of The Boring Company; co-founder of Neuralink; and co-founder and initial co-chairman of OpenAI, warned us about when he said: "AI will be the best or worst thing ever for humanity." Until AGI is developed, leveraging ANI (hereafter called AI for simplification) is the best way to command and control military systems. Weapons and warfighters with a better AI capability will have a distinct advantage over "less-smart," non-AI systems.

Twenty years ago, AI was rudimentary. For example, it was impossible to use a mobile phone for navigation and it would have been considered in the realm of science fiction to have such a small, battery-powered device provide point-to-point voice directions and display an interactive map to a person driving a car. Today, corporations are planning to deploy self-driving cars that will leverage AI to operate autonomously. What will happen two decades from now? New means of human to computer interface are poised to cause the next big disruption. Developments in the science of brain computer interface (BCI) promise to merge the warfighter with intelligent weapons, creating a speed of execution that is impossible today.

Humans and the technology loop

Until the late 20th century, most weapons were human operated, employing a human in the loop (HITL) mode where a human operator directed the operation and effects of the weapon. HITL weapons require human interaction to hit their mark and military forces exerted great efforts to train warfighters to wield them efficiently and effectively. For example, imagine an archer who fires an arrow at a target. The archer's skill, the capabilities of the bow and arrow, and environmental factors (such as the wind, the degree of illumination, the weather) determine whether the arrow hits the target. A skilled archer uses his mind to instinctively calculate these factors and apply an intuitive ballistic calculation to hit the target. When the archer decides, the arrow is loosed and flies where it was aimed. This is what an anti-tank gunner of an HITL weapon would do today, firing an unguided rocket-propelled grenade (RPG). The operator is smart; the missile is dumb.

The methods of war, however, are changing. Weapons can now be fired in the direction of the target and, using the AI targeting parameters embedded in the weapon, the projectile will find and engage the target independently. This process is called human on the loop (HOTL). Using the aforementioned analogy of the archer, an HOTL bow and arrow system allows the archer to release his arrow into the air and then, as the arrow nears the target (or targets), the arrow senses this and independently maneuvers within its capabilities to strike the highest value target and/or the optimum place to inflict the most damage. The AI embedded in the arrow would make this possible. This is generally what is done by many smart, anti-tank missiles today, such as the fire-and-forget FGM-148 Javelin anti-tank guided missile (ATGM). The Javelin is autonomously guided to the target after launch, leaving the gunner free to reposition or reload immediately. The operator is smart; the missile is smart.

Human out of the loop (HOOTL) involves intelligent, autonomous weapon systems that can independently search for and engage targets based on their AI programing to establish the engagement criteria and priorities. For a HOOTL

The tempo of war is accelerating and future engagements will be faster and more lethal than ever before. Screens, joysticks, and controllers will soon yield to more sophisticated brain computer interface options for training and operations. Recent developments in such technologies will soon enable human warfighters to control computers and weapons with their minds. (US Army Research Lab image).

system, the only purpose of the human operator is to turn the system on and off. The advantage of HOOTL weapons is their speed of action as decision making is executed at machine speed. In addition, HOOTL weapons can engage targets where it is too dangerous to send human-operated systems. With no humans at risk, the mission can still be accomplished and friendly lives can be spared. Continuing with the bow and arrow, the scene now changes dramatically. There is no archer and therefore no need for extensive human training and preparation; there is simply a bow with a quiver of arrows. The archery system is turned on and monitored by a human (who is not a trained archer). The system is triggered (arrows let loose) by a condition. Once activated, the HOOTL archery system launches arrows that may then loiter over an engagement area for as long as it takes to identify and descend to engage the target.

The HOOTL weapon system observes, orients, acquires, decides, and acts on its own, according to how it was programmed. It does not sleep; it has no fear; it never retreats and will continue if it has the power and resources to accomplish its designed function. Today, most naval close-in defense systems, and the best air defense weapon systems, such as the American Patriot Air Defense System, the Israeli Iron Dome, and the Russian S-300, 400 and 500 series missile systems, have fully autonomous modes. These systems are HOOTL weapons because they must react to threats faster than human operators can observe, orient, acquire, decide, and act. Another example of HOOTL systems in use today are vehicle protective systems such as the Trophy Active Protection System. Trophy is designed to protect vehicles from ATGMs, RPGs, and similar anti-tank munitions by automatically firing several projectiles at the incoming threat. Once turned on, Trophy must work autonomously as the speed of reaction required to defeat incoming missiles is beyond human capacity. The human operator only serves as a monitor because the weapon is artificially intelligent.

A fourth method of weapons control, tentatively labeled Human governing the loop (HGTL), is theorized. This method solves many of the ethical issues concerning HOOTL weapons by keeping a human involved in the process, but the means by which this human interface would be integrated is currently nascent. Since computers can operate at speeds beyond human cognition, HGTL requires an interface that goes beyond mouse, touch pad, or voice interaction. In short, to properly execute HGTL, humans will have to use a different means of supervision and will have to merge with AI.

Controlling the computer

The most recent development in leveraging AI for military applications is the development of new ways to interact with computers. Human control of computers has come a long way in a relatively short period of time. Computer keyboards for punch cards emerged in the 1930s but only became common in the 1970s. The trackball was developed in 1946 and used to control post-World War II weapon systems. The first computer mouse was developed in 1964 but did not come into everyday use until 1984 with the debut of the Macintosh 128K computer. The first computer voice user interface (VUI), that enabled users to interact with a device or application using spoken voice commands, began in 1952, but was not pervasive until recently with VUIs such as Amazon Alexa, Apple Siri, Google Assistant, Samsung Bixby, Yandex Alisa, and Microsoft Cortana. Touch pad technology, ubiquitous today, was not in widespread use until the commercial success of the iPad in 2010. In a similar fashion to these commercial devices, control interfaces for weapon systems have undergone an evolution that has reached the peak of man–machine HOTL capabilities. For many new military systems, the speed of reaction required for the most modern weapons to function at their fullest capacity demands new methods of control.

In 2019, the United States Defense Advanced Research Projects Agency (DARPA) began funding a program to develop a brain-to-machine interface for warfighters to control weapon systems through thought alone. This interface is in the form of a wearable headset that uses high-resolution, bidirectional, brain–machine interfaces. As stated by Al Emondi, the DARPA program manager:

> The Next-Generation Nonsurgical Neurotechnology (N3) program aims to develop high-performance, bi-directional brain-machine interfaces for able-bodied service members. Such interfaces would be enabling technology for diverse national security applications such as control of unmanned aerial vehicles and active cyber defense systems or teaming with computer systems to successfully multitask during complex military missions. Whereas the most effective, state-of-the-art neural interfaces require surgery to implant electrodes into the brain, N3 technology would not require surgery and would be man-portable, thus making the technology accessible to a far wider population of potential users. Noninvasive neurotechnologies such as the electroencephalogram and transcranial direct current stimulation already exist, but do not offer the precision, signal resolution, and portability required for advanced applications by people working in real-world settings.[2]

In short, DARPA's vision is to develop a wearable BCI to operate a computer. To achieve this, DARPA has challenged six teams to look at various ways to achieve BCI through exploring surgically, non-invasive interfaces and surgically, minutely invasive interfaces. In July 2019, the Battelle Memorial Institute, a research and development organization that manages eight national laboratories in the US, and is headquartered in Columbus, Ohio, was given a US$1 million award as part of DARPA's Artificial Intelligence Exploration program called Intelligent Neural Interfaces.

Neuralink's brain computer interface

Elon Musk plans to take the next step in human computer interface by creating a commercially available BCI. Musk created a neuroscience start-up company in 2016 called Neuralink to design and market a BCI implant. The purpose of the Neuralink implant is to connect human brains with computer interfaces through AI, eventually allowing human brains to merge with AI. "We're designing the first neural implant that will let you control a computer or mobile device anywhere you go. Micron-scale threads are inserted into areas of the brain that control movement. Each thread contains many electrodes and connects them to an implant, the Link." The Neuralink website explains that the "Link" is a sealed, implanted device that processes, stimulates, and transmits neural signals. Each small and flexible thread contains many electrodes for detecting neural signals. A compact, inductive charger wirelessly connects to the implant to charge the battery from the outside. The Link connects to a Neuralink app that allows the operator to control a device, keyboard and mouse directly with the activity of their brain, just by thinking about it.

On August 28, 2020, Musk held a Neuralink product demonstration to show how his Link, which is about the size of a large coin, can be safely implanted by replacing a piece of the human skull and wirelessly connecting with the human brain. He reported that the Link will be sold commercially and will solve important problems such as memory loss, hearing loss, depression, insomnia, blindness, paralysis, seizures, addiction, anxiety and other afflictions. It would be inserted in the patient's skull in an operation that would be conducted by a robotic, surgical system monitored by doctors. "It's like a Fitbit in your skull with tiny wires," Musk said of the device. Although initial plans are to help people with neural issues and spinal problems, Musk remarked that it will quickly expand in purpose for use by uninjured people who want

Elon Musk stands next to the robotic surgery machine that his company created to implant a new brain computer interface into a human's skull. Musk and others founded Neuralink, an American neurotechnology company, to develop implantable brain–machine interfaces. (Wikipedia)

to upgrade their cognitive capabilities. He expects to have the technology commercially available soon, but much work remains to be completed, and no date was given at the time. "The future is going to be weird."

The initial features of the Link are to monitor an individual's health and to connect to peripheral devices, such as a smart watch or phone. It was demonstrated on live pigs in Musk's product demonstration.[3] Musk envisions the Link can be implanted in a human, upgraded, or removed without any damage to the person receiving the implant—a totally reversible procedure that leaves only a small scar and is fundamentally unnoticeable. It would have a full day's battery life and would recharge at night. In the live demonstration, Musk revealed how the implant allowed a pig to transmit data across a wireless connection, allowing researchers to read brain activity. In addition, Musk expects to imprint directly onto the pig's brain, stimulating its brain neurons to teach the animal various actions. In July 2020, the Link reached an important milestone from the US Food and Drug Administration when it was granted a "Breakthrough Device" designation. He also stated that, eventually, it will be as inexpensive as laser eye surgery. At the time, Musk expected the first BCI to be implanted into a human within a year. He also believed it will "100 percent be used for gaming," which opens the possibility to use the Link for military simulations. It also has the potential to store memories and replay them on command. It is an obvious next step to use the Link's ability to control military computers and hardware. The first military adopters would most likely be special operation forces soldiers and pilots, but the military applications appear numerous. Musk mentioned the ability to use the Link in a future form to create super vision and possibly telepathic communication between implanted humans. Neuralink's efforts have essentially created "Pig 1.5" (if you consider a natural pig as version 1.0). With Musk's drive, energy and genius, it seems possible people will be upgraded to "Human 2.0."

When (not if) AI is melded with human capabilities, warfighters will wage combat at incredible speed. Future military training, planning, and operations will change dramatically as warfighters are embedded with BCI to use weapons linked to an AI warfighting network. Once the realm of science fiction, such as the 1982 techno-thriller *Firefox*, where a next-generation fighter aircraft was flown by a human that could pilot the machine with his mind, the development of BCI is moving closer to reality. Today, we are maximizing AI to enable weapons to operate faster than the speed of human cognition. Ray Kurzweil, Director of Engineering at Google, believes that for humans to control AI at such speeds requires merging with the AI. He remarked in 2017 that "by the 2030s we will connect our neocortex, the part of our brain where we do out thinking, to the cloud." If the current developments of DARPA's N3 program and Elon Musk's Neuralink continue to accelerate, it will soon be possible for soldiers to operate the latest military weapons with their minds alone.

Being able to operate at the speed of thought, creating a hybrid, human–computer–weapon interface, will create mind-boggling speeds of execution. With the proper BCI, training will be conducted in ways that may resemble what was fictionalized in *The Matrix*. In the same fashion, planning and rehearsals will be conducted and finalized in rapid time. War will become a combination of all four warfighting methods of control—HITL, HOTL, HOOTL, and HGTL. Humans will still be central to military operations, but the tempo of war is accelerating to the point where future battles will be hyper-fast and will require new means of supervision. Commanders will adopt AI-leveraged means to visualize the battlespace. Military forces that do not embrace the possibilities of BCI will look as if they are operating in slow motion, or standing still, compared to an opponent who embraces it. Future war will be executed at the speed of thought and only those swift enough to think and operate at machine speeds will be able to win the race.

The Fusion of Sensors and Shooters

"The Second Nagorno-Karabakh War demonstrated how the fusion of modern sensors and precision fires made it impossible to hide in the battlespace."

John Antal, lecture on the Second Nagorno-Karabakh War at the US Army Fires in MultiDomain Transformation Conference at Fort Sill, Oklahoma, September 2, 2021

This image depicts the target cycle of the Fire Shadow, a loitering munition weapon system, designed by US defense corporation Lockheed Martin. Although the United States pioneered loitering munitions, its military has been slow to adopt them. Currently there are no loitering munition units in the US Army. This will most likely change as the effectiveness of loitering munitions as an element of persistent long-range precision fires was proven during the Second Nagorno-Karabakh War in 2020. (Lockheed Martin image)

CHAPTER 11

Lessons from the Second Nagorno-Karabakh War

"Arrows, even especially painful Parthian ones, must run out at some point, thought the Romans."

FROM PLUTARCH'S *LIFE OF CRASSUS*

"I'm not convinced that we have fully thought our way through all of the challenges we may face on the future high-end battlefield if deterrence fails. We need to look harder at key cases, such as the Nagorno-Karabakh war between Armenia and Azerbaijan… Perhaps hardest of all, these changes must be made swiftly."

SECRETARY OF THE ARMY CHRISTINE WORMUTH, OCTOBER 11, 2021

Horses snorted, hooves pounded the ground, arrows zipped through the air, legionnaires prayed to their gods and cursed their general. The Parthians were all around them. The air was hot with fear and filled with a continuous barrage of deadly darts that never ceased. The Romans closed ranks, overlapped their shields to form the *testudo* formation and created a defensive wall against the enemy's missiles. This locked shield formation had worked so well in past battles against other opponents but was now proving to be only partially effective against these Parthian arrows. The arrows were barbed in a special way, and fired with such force from their small compound bows, that they punctured the large convex shields that characterized Roman tactical formations. When the Parthian horse archers then withdrew to collect more arrows from a mobile supply train that hovered just outside the zone of disruption, the enemy's heavy cavalry, the cataphracts, were upon the Romans; as Cassius Dio wrote, "with a rush, striking down some, and at least scattering the others; and if they (the Romans) extended their rank to avoid this, they would be struck with the arrows."

Ten thousand Parthians were attacking 43,000 Romans. The Roman general, Marcus Licinius Crassus, who was central to the defeat of Spartacus in Italy in 71 BC, seemed unable to grasp what was happening. He had led his army of seven legions into the deserts of Parthia, modern day Iran, with great confidence. When dust was seen on the horizon, his scouts reported a vast enemy army, all on horseback, all light cavalry, and no infantry. Crassus had 35,000 well-trained infantry and 4,000 cavalry under his command. Reports from his scouts indicated he outnumbered the Parthians by three or four to one. Most importantly, the Parthians had no infantry.

Crassus smiled. As the enemy's cavalry approached it appeared his scouts had been correct and the Parthian force consisted only of light horsemen, with none of the heavily armored cataphract knights the Romans dreaded. Suddenly, the sound of Parthian drums echoed across the battlefield. This unseen pounding unnerved the Romans. Then, the Parthian cavalry drew closer and the horsemen in the front ranks tore off their tunics and revealed their armor. The Parthians had masked their armor to deceive the Romans to appear that they were only a light cavalry force, masking their true capability.

Crassus, perplexed by this unexpected move, ordered his legions into line formation; then as the legions were nearly formed up, Crassus changed his mind and ordered them into a huge hollow square. Confused, his men reformed. As the cataphracts charged forward, swarms of horse archers rode to the flanks and rode around Crassus's men as they were forming into the square. Crassus watched as the dust swirled and arrows flew, but his disciplined men formed properly, and he expected his legions could absorb the enemy's initial assault. Once the enemy horse archers ran out of arrows, his legions would move on.

The Parthians, however, did not run out of arrows. The day wore on and Roman casualties mounted. The Parthian general, Rustaham Surena, also known as Eran Spahbodh Rustaham Suren-Pahlav, had a sharp mind and the ability to think differently. Not only did he know the quality of his horse-archers and the deadly capability of their arrows, but he understood the power of preparation. He prepared in advance to meet Crassus and defeat him on open ground, by fighting at a distance and never allowing the Romans to execute their deadly close-combat tactics. Surena added an immense supply train of camels to his army to carry thousands of additional arrows for his horse archers. Surena's horse archers had an almost unlimited supply of projectiles, and this allowed his Parthian horse-archers to maintain their fire at a ferocious rate. Arrows hammered Crassus's legions all day, without respite. Casualties mounted, and morale sank.

Crassus ordered his son, Publius, to lead a force of veteran Gallic cavalry, archers, and legionaries to charge and disrupt the enemy. The initial charge seemed to work, as the Parthians fled the battlefield. After a pursuit of several miles, Publius fell into a Parthian ambush. Not a Roman escaped from this ambush. For Surena, this was all part of the plan. The Parthians had feigned retreat to exploit the Roman tactics. Stripped of their cavalry, the Romans were at Surena's mercy. Back at the infantry square, the Romans despaired when a cataphract displayed the severed head of Publius on a spearpoint. Seeing this, Crassus fell to his knees in grief and could no longer command. The Parthians renewed their attack as more arrows rained down upon the Romans. Legionnaires fell. Others moved forward to fill the gaps in the ranks. The Romans could not strike back at the Parthians, but they held their ground and despaired as their numbers dwindled. As night fell, Surena broke off the attack. Sensing an opportunity to flee, and thinking only of their own survival, the Romans fit to walk, left their wounded on the field and withdrew. As the sun rose, Surena's horsemen killed the wounded Romans left behind and pursued those that fled. The withdrawal soon lost cohesion, turned to a rout, and it was every man for himself. Parthian horsemen slaughtered everyone they could find. Crassus and at least 30,000 legionaries died at the battle of Carrhae in 53 BC. This was the greatest defeat Rome suffered since the battle at Cannae against Hannibal in 216 BC.

Roman arms lost this battle for several reasons. First, Crassus's leadership was abysmal. He was arrogant and displayed no foresight. He did not understand his enemy, his own forces, the terrain, or the timing. Second, the Roman army, for all its reputation as a battle-winning force, was predominantly an infantry army that was excellent at close combat but lacked the mobility or long-range striking power for decisive action against a mounted enemy. The legions could slaughter the tribes in Gaul and Spain or break the "unbeatable" Macedonian phalanx in close combat, but against a mobile, cavalry-centric army, the Romans were at a severe disadvantage. The Parthians did not fight by the Roman rule book. Surena understood the methodical Roman way of war and exploited that knowledge by denying the Romans their close-combat advantage. Using the superb Parthian compound bow and an unlimited supply of hard-piercing arrows, Surena's horse archers fought from a distance, and the Romans could do nothing about it. For the Romans, Carrhae was a crushing defeat.

Fast forward to 2025–2030. No longer just an infantry-centric force, modern Western armies fight using multi-domain operations that employ joint and combined arms tactics. War is now multi-dimensional and hyper-fast and speeds up with every innovation in technology. As the convergence of technology with Artificial Intelligence (AI) increases, the velocity of military operations continues to escalate. The thought that military leaders today can learn anything from the ancient battlefield of Carrhae seems far-fetched.

This, however, is only a matter of perspective and, if you think differently, there are some stark lessons that cry out to the modern military leader from the ghosts of Carrhae. Just as the Romans were proud in their belief in their close-combat excellence at breaking the phalanx, their enemies were devising new ways to smash the legion. Today, US and NATO forces must quickly mobilize and move combat forces to react to a threat in Ukraine or an invasion of the NATO Baltic states (Latvia, Lithuania, and Estonia). In those battlespaces, NATO forces will most likely arrive at a numerical disadvantage. Once battle is engaged, the enemy will fight at a distance, using Unmanned Aerial Vehicles (UAVs) and Loitering Munitions (LMs), negating the close-combat expertise of US and NATO forces. The question that Carrhae echoes across the years is this: Do US and NATO forces have the mobile striking power to fight outnumbered and win against peer competitors in today's battlespace?

The lessons from Carrhae resonated in the mountains of Nagorno-Karabakh. The Azerbaijanis used clever tactics to swarm Armenian air defenses with drones and smash them with artillery and rockets. This high-tech top-attack brought down the Armenian army. Armenia was out-fought, out-numbered, and out-spent. They lost the war despite controlling the high-ground in a mountainous region that favored traditional defense. The Armenians had 26 years to prepare their mountain defenses, and they believed that the strength of these positions would deter any war or, if war broke out, would break the Azerbaijani assault. This defensive mentality, like the "Maginot Line" spirit of the French Army in 1940, infected the Armenian military. As with the German *blitzkrieg* against France, the Azerbaijani effort to seize Nagorno-Karabakh proved unstoppable. Remaining on the defensive, and without a clear intent to counterattack to defeat the Azerbaijanis, the Armenians lost critical systems, personnel, and precious time. Instead of recognizing the town of Shusha as decisive terrain and the center of gravity of the entire Nagorno-Karabakh effort, the Armenians failed to mount a serious defense to stop Azerbaijani *spetsnaz* (special forces) from infiltrating and capturing the town. Executing neither a "relative" or "absolute" defense of their mountain defenses,[1] the Armenian shield cracked and collapsed. To win the war, the Armenians needed to hold the mountains to gain time, then mobilize and launch a powerful counterattack against Azerbaijani forces in the open, low ground of the Aras river valley. This they could not do. When they lost their air defense, they surrendered the air domain and Azerbaijani drones interdicted Armenian movement. Frozen in their trenches, the Armenians could not maneuver or counterattack. Their attempts to widen the war using ballistic missiles against Azerbaijani cities failed. The Azerbaijani attack seized the initiative from the start of the war and maintained that initiative until Armenia surrendered.

That Azerbaijan won the war, especially with Turkey's help, is not extraordinary, considering the correlation of forces arrayed against the Republic of Artsakh and Armenia. What is exceptional is that this was the first modern war primarily decided by the cooperation of unmanned weapons and human forces in combat. This manned-unmanned teaming was a loose cooperation guided by the general principle to use the best robotic weapon or human force for the circumstance. Azerbaijani planners designated strike zones for Unmanned Combat Aerial Vehicles (UCAVs) and LMs to hunt targets according to their targeting parameters. Knocked off balance, the stunned Armenians clung to their defenses. Armenian forces recovered in time to ambush Azerbaijan armor attacking along the Lachin Corridor, but this did not halt the attack as the Azerbaijanis, once blocked, they deftly switched to an infiltration attack with light infantry. Azerbaijani *spetsnaz* infiltrated through Armenian lines in small groups, masking their movement in the forests and deep gorges to seize the decisive terrain and the center of gravity: the mountain-top city of Shusha. The cooperation of robotic systems and human soldiers tipped the balance in Azerbaijan's favor and took the Armenians by surprise.

The lessons offered by a thorough study of the Second Nagorno Karabakh War apply to the US and NATO forces today, as they provide insights into the conduct of modern war. Chief of the General Staff (CGS) of the British Army, Gen Sir Mark Carleton-Smith recognized this when he remarked on September 15, 2021: "The future character of conflict has already made itself apparent following recent campaigns around the world…specifically the conflict in Nagorno-Karabakh in 2020 between the armed forces of Armenia and Azerbaijan…saw the employment of precision strikes assets at operational depth, which was once thought to be the sole preserve of great powers."[2]

Here are fourteen lessons derived from a close study of the open-source information from the Second Nagorno-Karabakh War.

1. Know yourself and know your enemy. The First Nagorno-Karabakh War was a protracted conflict fought between 1988 and 1994. It ended with an Armenian victory and the occupation by Armenia of most of Nagorno-Karabakh. The Azerbaijanis did not want a repeat of that disaster. They partnered with Turkey and Pakistan to upgrade and train their military. The professionalism and competence the Azerbaijani military gained from this effort is a significant reason for their victory in the war in 2020. The Azerbaijanis also studied their opponent, the situation, and the timing. They researched

Armenia's military strengths and weaknesses, studied recent changes in the methods of war, and adopted the latest weapons and proven tactics from Turkey's experience in Syria and Libya. Azerbaijan planners recognized the situation by conducting a close study of the terrain and identifying Shusha as the decisive terrain and the center of gravity. Timing the attack to occur during a world-wide pandemic, particularly when COVID-19 was severely affecting the Armenian population, aided Azerbaijan and gained surprise. Mobilizing first and striking first was a key part of Azerbaijan's strategy. One of the primary lessons of the Second Nagorno-Karabakh War is to "know yourself and know your enemy," and act on that knowledge.

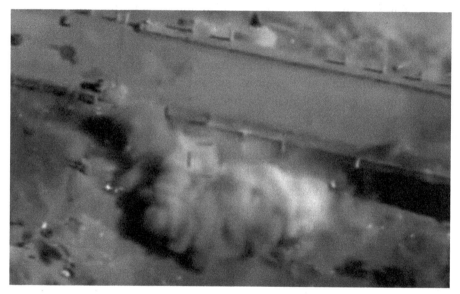

An Azerbaijani TB2 UCAV used smart micro-munitions to strike an Armenian position hiding under a bridge. (Image capture from Azerbaijani Ministry of Defense video)

2. Preparation. Azerbaijan prepared for the Second Nagorno-Karabakh War for decades before they launched the attack in September 2020. From the military perspective, Azerbaijan outspent Armenia six to one, investing more than $24–$42 billion in the latest UAV, UCAV, LM, ATGM, air defense and ballistic missile technology from Turkey and Israel. In the spring of 2020, Turkey trained Azerbaijani UAS operators prior to the start of the conflict. Turkey also closely advised Azerbaijani operators during the war. This vital preparation gained a niche advantage for Azerbaijan that they would use to win air dominance. Armenia learned of the qualitative and technological improvement of Azerbaijan's military before the war, but did not react in time, either from institutional lethargy, corruption, or hubris. Politically, Azerbaijan's alliance with Turkey, and close technological support from Israel, strategically isolated Armenia. In addition, Turkey's posturing on Azerbaijan's behalf influenced the Russians not to intervene on Armenia's side.

3. Strike First. Done right, a "first strike" is decisive. The first to move in multiple domains, and to integrate and synchronize fires and maneuver into a unifying concept, gains a tremendous advantage. Although Azerbaijan claimed Armenia started the fighting on September 27, 2020, and there may have been a mutual exchange of artillery fire, the Azerbaijanis were waiting for such an excuse to launch a powerful "counteroffensive," what they called Operation Iron Fist. Azerbaijan mobilized weeks before the fighting started and was ready to unleash Iron Fist at the slimmest provocation. In the opening days, using a clever combination of AN-2 Colt biplanes as remotely piloted vehicles (RPVs), Azerbaijan attacked the Armenian air defense network in Nagorno-Karabakh. Using World War II-era AN-2 aircraft as decoys to "turn on" the Armenian air defense radars, the Azerbaijanis then swarmed the Armenian air defense systems with LMs, UCAVs, and precision and non-precision fires. Azerbaijan disintegrated the Armenian air defense in the first few days of the war. Once Azerbaijan won air supremacy, their airborne robotic systems hunted targets inside the designated strike zones, day and night, at machine speeds. Armenia lost 1,021 vehicles destroyed or disabled in these attacks. Azerbaijani targeting parameters were, in priority: air defense, electronic warfare, command and control, artillery, tanks, armored vehicles, trucks, and troops. The side with a first-strike-advantage, and the ability to integrate and synchronize fires and maneuver into a unifying concept, gains surprise. This is what Azerbaijan achieved. Azerbaijan struck first and maintained the initiative throughout the war.

We can compare modern war to a game of five-dimensional chess, where each level is a separate but interconnected domain. In this analogy, US and NATO forces are almost always playing the black pieces and, therefore, move second. Since no country will have an unlimited supply of precision-guided weapons, especially UAS, preemption seems the best case in a use-them-or-lose-them situation. Russia's concepts of Seventh-generation Warfare, involving precision weapons, information warfare, cyber and electronic warfare, emphasizes the value of striking first to gain surprise.[3] An article in a leading Russian newspaper reported that Russian Rocket forces routinely practice "delivering preemptive strikes against mock enemies."[4] The Chinese People's Liberation Army embraces the same concept. They see the "launch of high-intensity strikes in a concealed and surprise fashion; and doing everything possible in the first strike to basically paralyze the enemy operational SoS (system of systems), and in one stroke seize the 'three dominances': 1. War control, and therefore, campaign success) depends on information dominance; 2. combat space is shrinking, but war space has expanded; and 3. target-centric warfare provides the means to defeat an adversary's operational system.[5] In this five-dimensional chess game, the Russians and Chinese will play the white pieces and move first. If done right, the first strike determines the outcome of future wars. Countering a first-move advantage, using everything from masking (see Lesson 8) to having a resilient and credible counterstrike capability, is the essence of deterrence in the 21st century.

4. War now moves at hyper-speed and is more connected that ever before.
The pace of battle is now extremely fast. During the Second Nagorno-Karabakh War, the speed of engagements within the designated strike zones happened as fast as the machines could sense, identify, and strike. In addition, Azerbaijani UAS operators observed attack results in real time, providing intelligence information and bomb-damage-assessment (BDA). As LMs and UCAVs shared targeting data, strikes shifted automatically to new, undamaged targets. Using unmanned systems, the kill-chain sped up.[6] Most kill-chains today have a human performing the "decide to attack" function. As the Human In The Loop (HITL) kill-chain transforms to an AI-leveraged Human On The Loop (HOTL), or Human Out Of The Loop (HOOTL) kill-web, the speed of combat will quicken beyond human cognition and humans will require the help of AI to synchronize the fight.

The speed of modern battle is driving important questions. Will we counter robots with robots, HOOTL with HOOTL, and develop a human-robot hybrid force? Will "blue" robotic drone hunters knock out incoming "red" LMs? Robotic systems represent a persistent threat that never sleeps, never wavers, never cowers, and never stops. This relentless pace of battle will break humans over time and disrupt human-centric combat formations. Although we are careful to keep a Human On The Loop for most military systems, there is no ethical problem with robots destroying robots. Military robots already fly in the air, roll across the terrain and slither into the ground. In the next few years, in a battlespace that is rapidly transforming to robotic systems, we will use a wide range of land, air, sea and space robots to "thicken" the force and enhance combat power.

Today, we cannot replicate the human brain. We cannot develop a machine that has the decision-making abilities, the ethical values, and the morals of a human. Someday, this may be possible, but most likely not for a while. Maximizing human potential involves using soldiers for their holistic cognitive intelligence rather than their muscle power. Today, the most capable force is human-centric, but reinforcing this force with robotic systems will add resilience and striking power. The Second Nagorno-Karabakh War demonstrated the power of such a hybrid human-robotic force. During the war, robotic systems pulverized the Armenian defenders and shaped the battlespace. Even with 26 years to prepare their trenches and bunkers, these traditional close-combat advantages did not benefit the Armenians. Despite their mountain defenses, the precision strikes from UCAVs and LMs negated the defender's advantage. Using LMs, UCAVs and precision fires, the offense is now in the ascendency. Major powers are investing time, money, and technology to develop hybrid human-robotic forces and more systems will transition from HITL to HOOTL control.

5. Dominate as many domains as possible. Azerbaijan dominated the land, air, space, and cyber domains for decisive moments to devastate Armenian forces and win the war. The sea domain was not a factor, as Nagorno-Karabakh is land-locked. Armenia quickly lost the air domain, fought in the land and cyber domains, but never dominated a single domain. In the past, it was difficult to dominate the land domain without control of the air and, often, the sea. Add the potential of space and cyber domains and the control of any one domain, without support from another, is in question. The ability to think, see, decide, and fight in multiple domains, and dominate the ones that matter for a particular time, is the essence of war in the 21st century. Add informational and the electro-magnetic spectrums as background factors that impact all domains, and the complexity of modern war increases. Fighting in all domains does not guarantee success in war, but it provides significant advantages.

Using the analogy of our five-dimensional chess game, with five chessboards possessing a full complement of black and white pieces on each board connected to place one board over the other, the complexity of modern war is apparent. Any piece, a queen, for instance, might move across the five planes to attack from the top board to the bottom, from the fourth board to the third. This analogy applies to multi-domain operations. Cross-domain maneuver along the five domains of multi-domain warfare provides the concentration of power on one plane that can be overwhelming. Add to this the impact of information war, which is not recognized as a separate domain, but which affects all domains, and the ability to see the enemy and their own forces in the full electromagnetic spectrum, which effects all domains, and you understand the definition of concentration of force in 21st-century warfare. Azerbaijan used Turkish satellites and accessed commercial satellites for data transmission and information to prepare for the war before the actual fighting began. Once the war started, Azerbaijan commanded the land, air, space, and cyber domains for decisive moments during the first two weeks of the fighting to devastate Armenian air defenses, and this gave Azerbaijan air supremacy over Nagorno-Karabakh. From that moment on, the Azerbaijanis continued to fight in all domains to their advantage. The ability to see, decide, and engage in multiple domains, and dominate the ones that matter during decisive periods, is the essence of war in the 21st century.

The Mini-Harpy Loitering Munition is a smaller version of the Harop "kamikaze" drone produced by the Israel Aerospace Industries. The Harop, which can operate autonomously, was successfully employed by Azerbaijan during the war as long-range precision fires across the depth and width of the strike zone to attack high value targets. The system has full mission capabilities that range from search, through attack and battle damage assessment. The Mini-Harpy "kamikaze" loitering munition is fully autonomous, has a range of about 100 kilometers (62 miles), carries up to an 8-kilogram (17.6lb) warhead, and will provide a close-in "sensor and strike" capability that is less expensive than the larger Harop, but as precise and lethal. (IAI illustration).

6. Use fires to maneuver instead of maneuver to fire. The war was won by Azerbaijan with precision stand-off weapons, primarily artillery and drones, and the daring assaults of their human-centric maneuver forces. Azerbaijan won air supremacy with its drone fleet in the first week of the war and then maneuvered ground forces to occupy key terrain and critical objectives.

The Armenians fought bravely and contested the battlespace, but the odds quickly stacked against them. Armenians inflicted heavy casualties on the Azerbaijani ground forces in several engagements, but the Armenians could not counter the drones and the battlespace was shaped by UCAVs, LMs, and UAVs spotting for artillery, before the ground engagements occurred. Most of the casualties inflicted upon the Armenians were from TB2 UCAVs that launched smart micro-munitions, the HAROP "kamikaze" LMs, and other UAVs that designated targets for UCAVs, LMs, and long-range artillery.

Electronic Warfare (EW) "fires" also played an important role, jamming Armenian air defenses prior to Azerbaijani drone assaults. There are reports that Turkish KORAL EW systems were used to prepare the battlespace for UCAV and LM attacks. These are the same tactics that the Turkish military perfected in Syria and Libya.

The Azerbaijanis waged a high-speed air assault, but a slow-grinding ground attack, maneuvering precision fires and then attacking with ground forces. The ground forces took several weeks to secure about 100 kilometers in the southern low-lands of Nagorno-Karabakh, before turning north to take key terrain along the Lachin Corridor and the strategic town of Shusha. This deliberate approach resulted from many factors—Armenian opposition, the training level of the Azerbaijani Army, the desire to minimize friendly casualties, and the political uncertainty of Russia's next move—but the pace of advance rested upon the success of the drone war. As Azerbaijan gained air supremacy and disintegrated the Armenian ability to execute combined arms warfare by destroying air defense, command and control, electronic warfare and artillery systems, the pace of the advance sped up. Throughout this effort, the Azerbaijanis method was to employ precision fires to enable ground force maneuver. The "shaping battle" fought by Azerbaijan's unmanned systems set up the ground advance and enabled the successful infiltration attack that seized Shusha and won the war.

7. The battlespace is transparent. Sensors, the most important ones mounted in satellites, aircraft, and UAVs, gave the Azerbaijani military a clear, 24-hour, unblinking view of the battlespace. Optical, thermal, and electronic sensors identified Armenian positions that were camouflaged in the traditional way.

Turkey's AWACs systems, the Boeing 737 AEW Peace Eagle, used advanced radar to track airborne and ground targets simultaneously across the battlespace. According to Russian sources, the Peace Eagle relayed Armenian target information to the Azerbaijani and Turkish drone operators. Once the targets were located, the TB2s and HAROPs observed, tracked, and destroyed targets automatically. These systems and others that were observing the strikes relayed videos of the attacks in real-time. High-definition, full-motion-real-time videos from these platforms provided ISR, destroyed systems and personnel, and provided accurate battle damage assessments (BDA). In multiple videos, after an Armenian MRLS would launch its rockets, a TB2 would film the systems withdrawal back to a rearming and resupply area, often hidden in forests. When enough Armenian systems arrived in the rearming area, multiple LMs

The General Atomics MQ-9 Reaper is a Medium Altitude Long Endurance (MALE) Unmanned Combat Aerial Vehicle (UCAV) used by the US military and several allied countries. It can carry a wide range of sophisticated missiles, including the HELLFIRE Missile and Intelligence Surveillance and Reconnaissance (ISR) packages. The cost of each MQ-9 is difficult to estimate, particularly since the system normally operates in groups of four and are usually sold in packages of four or more but is around SU$30.2 million each. The REAPER requires an extensive infrastructure and human support team to keep it flying. It has been in service since 2007. The Bayraktar TB2, according to an August 2021 European Interoperability Center report, cost only US$1–2 million each. (US Air Force image)

and UCAVs would attack. In these videos, the destruction of several Armenian launchers and supply trucks occurred in seconds.

Although both sides in the Second Nagorno-Karabakh War had plenty of tanks, tanks rarely moved within shooting range of each other. During the war, there were more casualties from standoff engagements than from close-combat fights. Tanks are a vital part of modern war, as no other system combines mobility, firepower and protection to such a degree, but tank systems and tactics must change. Unprotected tanks that are not masked from enemy sensors are vulnerable to attack by long range precision fires from ATGMs, LMs, and UCAVs. The one exception was the battle of Shusha where Azerbaijani *spetsnaz* defeated Armenian tank attacks with shoulder-fired ATGMs. Combined arms can still be decisive, as air platforms cannot take and hold ground, but only if ground forces survive long enough to move within direct fire range.

8. Masking is essential to survive in today's battlespace. During the war, the Armenians could not hide. One anonymous Armenian soldier said in a video interview during the war: "We cannot hide, and we cannot fight back." Traditional physical camouflage was used to obscure key weapons platforms, which was ineffective against sensors that registered thermal and electronic signatures. Unable to mask from enemy sensors and precision strikes, Armenian morale and will to fight plummeted.

Traditional camouflage is no longer enough, although all US And NATO units should become experts at camouflage. US and NATO forces must adopt the concept of "masking" in everything they do. Masking is the full-spectrum, multi-domain effort to deceive enemy sensors and disrupt enemy targeting. Masking involves all active and passive means to confuse, disaggregate, disrupt, jam, and deceive the enemy's sensors and disrupt the enemy's targeting network. This will require discipline, leadership, and new tactics, techniques, and procedures (TTP). Units must become expert at camouflaging in all environments. Discipline is required to enforce camouflage standards and leadership is needed to ensure that soldiers do not carry personal mobile phones into the battlespace. The thermal and electronic signatures of every system need to be diminished. Units should be able to go "dark" by turning off their electronic systems and operating for periods with no electronic emissions. Masking will require fresh thinking and innovative systems that minimize optical, thermal, and electronic signatures and the concept should be considered as a key element of war, as it is more than camouflage and security, and it permeates and enables all the other factors. The concept of masking is so important that military doctrine writers should make "masking" a separate principle of war. In the modern battlespace you either mask or die.

9. Top-attack is a decisive method of engagement. The proliferation of affordable and effective top-attack systems, as exemplified by the TB2 and Harop, is a significant trend. It is no longer necessary to have a big cannon to penetrate the front glacis of a tank's armor if you can destroy the tank with great accuracy from the top. Videos confirm Azerbaijani top-attack UAS strikes destroyed as many as 185 Armenian tanks, 89 armored fighting vehicles, 182 artillery guns, 73 multiple rocket launchers, 45 air defense systems, and 450 other vehicles. These video records, that were analyzed in detail by defense analyst Stijn Mitzer, publishing on the *Oryx* blog, claim 1,020 Armenian vehicles destroyed by unmanned systems or with the use of artillery enabled by unmanned systems.[7] The scale of these strikes by unmanned systems is stunning and unprecedented. In the long counterinsurgency wars of the past 20

Armenian towed howitzers were easy prey for Azerbaijan's TB2 UCAVs and LMs. How will towed artillery, no matter how well camouflaged, survive on the modern battlefield? In this photo, US Army towed howitzers conduct firing drills at the Joint Multinational Readiness Center in the Hohenfels Training Area, Germany from October 17-30, 2021. The exercise is designed to facilitate the brigade commander's gated training strategy to build lethal units in a kinetic, simulated combat scenario against a thinking opposing force. (U.S. Army photo by Staff Sgt. John Yountz)

years, insurgents attacked vehicles from the bottom with improvised explosive devices (IEDs). The IEDs now fly, and the top of an armored vehicle is the Achilles' heel of modern war.

10. Layered air defense and Active Protection at AI speeds are vital to survival. Armenia did not have a modern, Integrated Air Defense System (IADS). A modern IADS is far more complex than a singular SAM battery or its associated command vehicle and radar. Modern air defenses are layered with short and long-range weapons, integrated with air surveillance, battle management and weapons control, protected from multi-domain attacks, and capable of defeating all UAS threats. The mix of these layers matters. To stop a broad range of threats, the layered air defense network must defeat drones, helicopters, aircraft, and missiles. To survive, key platforms must have active protection that can disrupt, deflect, or confuse incoming direct-fire and top attack munitions with either on-board or complimentary systems. Current systems, such as the M1 Abrams tank, have reached their maximum weight and the limit of unused turret surface area. There just is simply no more capacity to add equipment to the top of the tank. Unmanned systems could provide active protection to legacy platforms to enhance survivability. A mobile "Iron Dome-like" top attack protection capability is imperative to defeat precision top attack munitions, missiles, aircraft munitions, and low-speed and high-speed threats.

The Second Nagorno-Karabakh War highlighted the requirement to defeat top-attack munitions. Most active protection systems, like the Israeli-made TROPHY system, do not protect armored vehicles from top-attack munitions. To survive in this new environment, a layered, multi-capable, full-spectrum, air defense against top attack munitions, missiles, aircraft, and low-speed and high-speed threats, is vital. The lesson is that survival in future wars will require a "spherical defensive system," a 360-degree mobile protective bubble. Active defenses are required to protect vehicles and personnel from underneath, lateral and top attack. This will require new systems and will represent a significant investment by military forces. Ground and air robotic systems that complement the defense of manned-systems could provide many of these capabilities.

11. Winning the information war. Both sides waged an information campaign against the other, but Azerbaijan and Turkey prevailed through their use of full-motion video footage from UAS and precision-guided munitions. The images of Armenian air defense platforms, artillery, tanks, infantry fighting vehicles, and troops being decimated in these videos played on all available social media outlets. Videos showed many of Armenia's Russian-made air defense systems with their radars spinning just before a Harop or smart-micro munition blew the system to pieces. Videos of Azerbaijan LMs striking equipment and troops were in full color, grisly and visceral. These short videos exemplified how Armenia was losing the war and that Armenia could do nothing to stop the Azerbaijani attacks. The impact of these videos negatively influenced Armenian morale and contributed to Armenia's surrender and capitulation to cease-fire terms. These videos also became a successful marketing message for Israel and Turkey's growing unmanned systems industry. On October 8, 2021, Bayraktar, the company that designed and manufactured the TB2 UCAV, announced contracts to thirteen countries.[8] TB2s and Harop LMs are now the hottest items on the international weapons market. At a cost of US$1–2 million each, the TB2 offers a combat-proven UCAV that even middle-tier

Rocket artillery is a vital component of the long-range fires that dominate the modern battlespace. The BM30/9K58/9A52-2 Smerch (Russian for tornado or whirlwind) is a 300 mm multiple rocket launcher (MRL) produced by Russia and used by both Armenia and Azerbaijan in the Second Nagorno-Karabakh War. The 9K58 Smerch can fire 12 rounds within 38 seconds to launch a devastating fusillade of missiles, with high explosive or cluster munition warheads, to a range of 90 kms. Before the war in 2020, Armenian layered rocket artillery was the main concern of the Azerbaijan General Staff. During the first weeks of the war, and after disintegrating the Armenian air defense network, Azerbaijan's drones targeted Armenian command posts and artillery. At least four Armenian Smerch MRLs were destroyed by Azerbaijani drones during the war. (Azerbaijan Ministry of Defense photo)

powers can afford.[9] On October 26, 2021, Ukrainian Armed Forces destroyed a pro-Russian separatist howitzer in the Donbass with missiles fired from a Bayraktar TB2. The Ukrainians used the video footage from this attack to show off their new capabilities and as another round in the information war against the pro-Russian forces. Drones and loitering munitions have come of age both as precision weapons and as important tools to fight and win information wars.

12. The Kill Chain is increasing in speed and will transform to an AI-enabled Kill Web. A Kill Chain is a military concept that describes the structure that connects sensors, shooters, and command-and-control nodes. The standard kill chain comprises the following steps: identify the target; dispatch the force to the target; decide to strike the target; then track, launch, hit the target, and assess the damage. Most kill chains operate at human decision-making speeds and at multiple echelons of command, using a human in the loop (HITL) command-and-control hierarchy. An example of a kill chain is the use of an MQ-9 Reaper armed with Hellfire Missiles to destroy a high-value target. In the past twenty years, the US and NATO nations have used unmanned systems primarily to hunt high-value targets. The strategically important assassination of Islamic Revolutionary Guard Corps (IRGC) commander Qasem Soleimani on January 3, 2020, by a US MQ-9 Reaper is an excellent example. This scale of this attack, however, is miniscule compared to the drone swarms that China and Russia are contemplating. During the Second Nagorno-Karabakh War, the Azerbaijani Kill Chain was extremely fast because of the use of sense-and-strike Harop[10] and Orbiter[11] LMs and TB2 UCAVs. By designating strike zones (free-fire zones) over Nagorno-Karabakh, the Azerbaijani systems observed and attacked targets without significant delays. Loitering munitions, such as the Harop and Orbiter, often attacked autonomously (HOOTL attacks), taking the human out of the loop and executing the strikes at machine speeds. These systems dramatically shortened the time to sense and strike the target, speeding up the kill chain.

A "kill web" is the military concept of a warfighting network that uses AI to synchronize the IoBT (Internet of Battlefield Things) to deliver cross-domain effects in real-time in a designated slice of the battlespace. A kill web operates at machine speeds in real time with Human On The Loop (HOTL) or Human Out Of The Loop (HOOTL) control. A "micro" example of a kill web is the network that targets, tracks, and fires the MK-15 Phalanx to defend ships and fixed points, the Counter-Rocket, Artillery, Mortar (C-RAM) or the Israeli-made Iron Dome. Abishur Prakash, the author of *The Age of Killer*

Azerbaijan media declared the Bayraktar TB2 as the "Conqueror of Karabakh" in an article posted on September 28, 2021, (https://aze.media/the-conqueror-of-karabakh-the-bayraktar-tb2/). The article claims: "In the course of this short but intense conflict, a handful of Azerbaijani Bayraktar TB2 UCAVs essentially broke the back of the Armenian military, destroying a confirmed total of 549 ground targets including 126 armored fighting vehicles (including 92 T-72 tanks), 147 artillery pieces, 60 multiple rocket launchers, 22 surface-to-air missile (SAM) systems, six radar systems and 186 vehicles… only two Azerbaijani Bayraktar TB2s were confirmed to have been lost to Armenian fire (one crashed, the other likely shot down) during the course of the war." TB2s are now sold to 13 countries. (Ukrainian Ministry of Defense).

Robots, believes "AI (Artificial Intelligence) and robotics will smash the status quo that exists in the world today and will reduce the gap between advanced military powers and the rest of the world."[12] Soon, AI-enabled kill webs will connect with every sensor and shooter in range and once given targeting parameters, will execute strike operations within a designated strike zone at machine speeds.

13. Unmanned Systems working with Humans are a Vital Part of Modern Warfare. In preparation for the Second Nagorno-Karabakh War, Azerbaijan purchased hundreds of unmanned systems. Azerbaijan used these unmanned systems, primarily the TB2 UCAV, and the Harop and Orbiter LMs, to project extended precision strikes into the entire depth of Nagorno-Karabakh.

Hunting targets 24/7, these unmanned systems dominated the battlespace. Inside designated strike zones, Azerbaijan operated their UAVs in Human On The Loop (HOTL) mode. LMs, however, were predominately HOOTL inside the strike zone. The combination of HOTL and HOOTL, combined with the maneuver of human forces, established a tempo of battle that overwhelmed the Armenians. Azerbaijan set the conditions with robotic systems, then finished the fight with soldiers. Their *spetsnaz* used masking to conduct the infiltration attack to capture Shusha, which was both the decisive terrain of Nagorno-Karabakh and the Center of Gravity of Armenian forces.

14. Executing and training Mission Command in a degraded or denied environment is vital. Azerbaijan's UAS hunted Armenian command and control (C2) headquarters and disrupted the Armenian C2 network from the first day of the war. Concurrently, Azerbaijani EW jammed Armenia's military communication networks. Turkish AWACs helped locate Armenian forces in the battlespace, giving drone operators precise locations of nearly all Armenian forces in Nagorno-Karabakh. In a denied and degraded battlespace, Armenia could not command its forces. Armenian forces seemed paralyzed by the pace of the Azerbaijani attack and many units stayed in their positions, waiting for orders that seldom came. Azerbaijan and Armenia did not execute mission command, but the Azerbaijani *spetsnaz* manifested the essence of mission command during their attack on Shusha. During this operation, Azerbaijani special forces soldiers infiltrated in small groups, seized key objectives in the town of Shusha and held against repeated Armenian counterattacks. An infiltration attack requires leaders to act on their own initiative to accomplish the higher commander's intent when communications with headquarters are impossible. Although they might not use the term, the Azerbaijani *spetsnaz* clearly executed "Mission Command" in the attack on Shusha.

Mission command has become the command philosophy of the US Army, but with mixed success, as few leaders seem to understand and practice the concept. US and NATO forces recognize that individual initiative by military leaders speeds up the decision-making process during combat and is essential to conducting multi-domain operations. Individual leader training and initiative are key. Mission command relies on the disciplined initiative of individual leaders to observe, orient, decide and act (OODA loop) in time, even when they cannot communicate with their higher commander. The US Army states that mission command "is the exercise of authority and direction by the commander using mission orders to enable disciplined initiative within the commander's intent to empower agile and adaptive leaders in the conduct

Israel's UVision's unique Hero line of High Precison Loitering Munition systems can loiter above a target and strike precisely when the opportunity arises, even if the target appears for only an instant. The smart loitering systems' unique cruciform aerodynamic configuration enables beyond line-of-sight capabilities and high levels of maneuverability. Featuring complete connectivity to existing Command, Control, Communication, and Computers (C4) systems, Hero's advanced datalink and real-time intelligence deliver up-to-the-minute situational awareness to all military echelons – from the individual soldier to central command – for tactical, operational and strategic targets. UVision-USA is currently engaged with US Special Forces, USMC, and the US Army on various programs. (Photo by UVision)

of Unified Land Operations." The six principles of mission command are: 1) Build cohesive teams through mutual trust; 2) Create shared understanding; 3) Provide a clear commander's intent; 4) Exercise disciplined initiative; 5) Use mission orders; and 6) Accept prudent risk.[13] The concept of decentralized execution exploits the human element and emphasizes trust, force of will, initiative, judgment, and creativity. Successful mission command demands that subordinate leaders at all echelons exercise disciplined initiative and act aggressively and independently to accomplish the mission. They focus their orders on the purpose of the operation rather than on the details of how to perform assigned tasks. Essential to mission command is the thorough understanding of the commander's intent at every level of command and a command climate of mutual trust and understanding. The intent of mission command is to empower leaders to continue to act decisively when they no longer have direct communications with their superiors. Rather than wait for orders that may never come in time, mission command expects leaders to act upon the commander's intent to accomplish the mission.

Conclusion—Learning from Other Wars

The Romans failed to learn from the lessons of the battle of Carrhae and never subdued the Parthians. Four hundred and thirty-one years later, at the battle of Adrianople on August 9, 378 AD the Romans suffered the worst military defeat in their long history. As at the battle of Carrhae, enemy horse archers pelted Roman infantry with arrows until the Romans broke. Estimated losses at Adrianople were even greater than at Carrhae.

> *Fires without Maneuver are Indecisive*
>
> New precision weapons make the modern battlespace more lethal, but fires without maneuver are indecisive

The Second Nagorno-Karabakh War offers insights into the changing methods of war. Unmanned systems, especially UCAVs and LMs, provide anyone with the money to buy them a new and effective means to deliver precision strikes from the air. However, the Second Nagorno-Karabakh War also showed that drones alone cannot win wars. Bad weather, effective air defense, and CUAS could have worked against the Azerbaijanis, however the weather remained good enough for Azerbaijan to win before the winter snows froze the battle lines. The Armenian air defense was not effective against the Azerbaijani UAS onslaught, and the few modern Russian-made CUAS systems the Armenians possessed, and their man-portable air defense missile systems, proved ineffective. For Azerbaijan, drones set the conditions for success, but it took well-trained and aggressive ground forces to seize the decisive terrain and secure the center of gravity. New precision weapons make the modern battlespace more lethal, but fires without maneuver are indecisive.

Drones and LMs are proliferating around the world as a means to provide a faster kill-chain to deliver precision strikes. Peer-threat militaries, such as Russia and China, recognize the impact of drones and LMs on the changing methods of warfare and are investing in drones and UCAVs. Russia and China intend to employ these "new" weapons in much the same way as Azerbaijan did during the Second Nagorno-Karabakh War, only on a larger scale. "The Russian arms industry has produced a number of LMs and deploying these to their top-tier combat units. Russia plans to put two different loitering munitions into serial production—the Kub and Lancet. Aside from television and thermal imaging cameras and radar transparent material, which are considered usual for such flying munitions, the electric-powered Kub and Lancet are supposed to be silent. Also of particular note, the article mentions that these systems will not just be available for domestic purchase, but also for foreign customers."[14]

The lessons and imperatives described above identify the key combat trends from a careful study of the Second Nagorno-Karabakh War. They also provide the elements for the creation of case studies to test future concepts in thought experiments, war-games, and simulations against a full spectrum of military threats. It seems self-evident that to ignore the lessons of the Second Nagorno-Karabakh War and assume through hubris or cultural bias that this conflict is not worthy of our study is insane. As the Secretary of the US Army said in October 2021: "We need to look harder at key cases, such as the Nagorno-Karabakh War."

Foresight is a vital skill for military leaders. One of the best ways to develop foresight is to study war, in depth and breadth, and understand how warfare changes. Recent surprises such as the pandemic, the brutal takeover of Hong Kong, the fiasco in Afghanistan, and the debut of Chinese hypersonic missiles circling the globe point to a lack of foresight. Foresight is the ability to fix problems in the short term and develop solutions for the long run. Russian General Valery Vasilyevich Gerasimov, Chief of the General Staff of the Armed Forces of Russia, and first Deputy Defense Minister, expressed the need for foresight in an article in "Military Industrial Courier" (Военно-промышленный курьер) in 2013: "As the nature of the war… is very difficult to foresee today… Any scientific research in the field of military science is worthless if military theory does not provide the function of foresight."

The Second Nagorno-Karabakh War has a similar significance to western military forces today as the impact of the 1973 Yom Kippur War did during the 1970s and 1980s. The lessons of the 1973 war influenced the development of tactics and weaponry during the Cold War and beyond. For example, the US military's thorough study of the war led to the AirLand Battle doctrine, and new systems, the "Big 5"—the M1 Main Battle Tank, Bradley Infantry Fighting Vehicle, Apache helicopter, Black Hawk helicopter, and Patriot Air Defense System. These warfighting platforms, although significantly upgraded, remain the mainstay of the US Army's striking power today. What can US and NATO forces do to prepare for the coming storm of the next war? Here are some ideas: Adopt masking in everything. Train rigorously to deceive enemy sensors and disrupt enemy targeting. Put commanders in charge of this effort and supply them with the means to achieve both deception and disruption. Rapidly field integrated air defense systems that can kill drones at HOOTL speeds. Develop the tactics, techniques, and procedures (TTP) for combat, combat support, and combat service support units to fight and win in this new transparent battlespace. Practice these capabilities in constructive, virtual, and live simulations. Field air-transportable expeditionary forces equipped with Loitering Munition (LM) and smart-mine top-attack area denial systems to reinforce allies in time to deter potential aggressors or, if deterrence fails, hold off the enemy and gain time. Develop and employ AI to synchronize all friendly UAS at machine speeds but keep humans governing the kill web. Transform the current command post architecture to execute mission command from distributed, mobile, masked, survivable protected command groups that operate within a dynamic, all domain, and resilient mesh network. In short, use the lessons of the Second Nagorno-Karabakh War to improve deterrence and, if deterrence fails, to win the next fight. This is a tall order. Our recent history of avoiding surprise has been poor. This must change. To do so will take serious thought, dialogue, hard work, funding, and new equipment, but most of all, it will take foresight.

Are US And NATO Forces Ready?

"The question on the minds of many western military leaders should ask is how well-prepared are their forces for modern combat as demonstrated during the Second Nagorno-Karabakh War? Would NATO combat units fare any better than the Armenians under a similar, unmanned whirlwind? Has NATO fielded the integrated air defense capability to counter UAV and LM assaults? How many NATO units have recently trained against UAV and LM swarm attacks? How will NATO integrate the command-and-control cross-domain capabilities of 29 multinational, multi-service UAV systems? These questions demand answers. Tackling this challenge should start with a detailed study of the Second Nagorno-Karabakh War to derive lessons learned, and then transform those lessons into updated doctrine, training, and equipment."

John Antal on US Army Futures Command podcast,
"Top Attack: Lessons Learned from the Second Nagorno-Karabakh War," April 1, 2021

Timeline of the Second Nagorno-Karabakh War

1988–1994: The First Nagorno-Karabakh War was a six-year conflict fought between Armenia and Azerbaijan. Azerbaijan suffered a series of humiliating defeats. Armenia won the war and a ceasefire was agreed to in 1994. According to the Congressional Research Service (CRS) report *Azerbaijan and Armenia: The Nagorno-Karabakh Conflict*, "Observers estimate the conflict resulted in around 20,000 deaths and more than 1 million displaced persons. The displaced included about 500,000 Azerbaijanis from areas surrounding Nagorno-Karabakh and the region itself, about 185,000 Azerbaijanis from Armenia, and more than 350,000 Armenians from Azerbaijan." The victorious Armenians declared Nagorno-Karabakh as an independent state, the Republic of Artsakh, with its capital as Stepanakert. Artsakh was not recognized as an independent state by the rest of the world.

1992: On May 15, 1992, six post-Soviet states belonging to the Commonwealth of Independent States—Russia, Armenia, Kazakhstan, Kyrgyzstan, Tajikistan, and Uzbekistan—sign the Collective Security Treaty, also called the "Tashkent Pact" establishing the Collective Security Treaty Organization (CSTO). The CSTO is a Russian version of NATO where an attack on one is considered an attack on all. Russia, however, has never considered Nagorno-Karabakh as part of Armenia and, therefore, an attack on Nagorno-Karabakh did not trigger the CSTO alliance.

1993: Three other post-Soviet states—Azerbaijan, Belarus, and Georgia—join the Tashkent Pact and the treaty took effect in 1994.

1994: The Organization for Security and Cooperation in Europe (OSCE) establishes the Minsk Group in 1994 to facilitate peace talks. The United

States, France, and Russia serve as co-chair countries, but nothing is resolved. The OSCE would work for 26 years and accomplish nothing. See Adam Ereli, "The Minsk Group and the Failure of Multilateral Mediation," *The Washington Times*, September 27, 2021, https://www.washingtontimes.com/news/2021/sep/27/minsk-group-and-failure-multilateral-mediation/

1999: Azerbaijan, Georgia, and Uzbekistan withdraw from the Tashkent Pact–CSTO.

2002: Russia, Armenia, Kazakhstan, Kyrgyzstan, Tajikistan, and Uzbekistan agree to create the CSTO as a military alliance.

2013: Russia starts delivering US$1 billion in arms to oil-rich Azerbaijan. Cash-strapped Armenia primarily relies on Russian credit to upgrade its military forces. (Reuters)

2016: Tensions rise as border incidents increase between Azerbaijan and Armenia, and the self-proclaimed Republic of Artsakh, over Nagorno-Karabakh. "200 reported casualties" and in Azerbaijan gaining control of two strategic heights in previously Armenian-held territory. Russian mediation helps to establish a new ceasefire agreement. (CRS report)

2018: Nikol Vovayi Pashinyan (born June 1, 1975) declares a "Velvet Revolution" against the Armenian government and leads demonstrations that force the sitting prime minister and president, Serzhik Azati Sargsyan, to resign. Sargsyan had been in power for a decade and had become increasingly unpopular with many Armenians. Pashinyan was elected as prime minister of Armenia on May 8, 2018.

2019: Azerbaijan is angered by Armenia's hosting the pan-Armenian games in Stepanakert, the capital city of Nagorno-Karabakh, the Republic of Artsakh. In August 2019, in response to Azerbaijani comments about Artsakh, Pashinyan declares in a speech that Nagorno-Karabakh "belongs to Armenia, period." According to a November 6, 2019, report in *Eurasia.net*, under Pashinyan, Armenia has seen a significant improvement in democracy, freedom of the press, fighting corruption, and its economy improved to be one of the fastest growing among post-Soviet Union countries. Nevertheless, a land-locked country with no oil wealth (compared to Azerbaijan), Armenia is dependent upon Russia for trade, energy, employment, and regional security.

2020

June 22: According to the Azerbaijani Ministry of Defense: "In accordance with the combat training plan for 2020 approved by the Minister of Defense, units of the Azerbaijan Army conducted exercises to work out tasks for planning and conducting offensive operations in mountainous terrain. The exercise involved up to 800 servicemen, about 100 units of armored vehicles, about 40 artillery mounts of various calibers, and six combat and transport helicopters. The purpose of the exercise was to improve the combat skills of commanders in mountainous terrain, to manage units during offensive operations in the mountains, to check the physical endurance of military personnel, and to organize unit interoperability."

July: According to *Kommersant*: "After the completion of the next Turkish-Azerbaijani exercises in July–August, a significant group of the Turkish Armed Forces allegedly remained on the territory of Azerbaijan, which was called upon to play a coordinating and directing role in planning and conducting an offensive operation in Nagorno-Karabakh. We are talking about 600 servicemen, including a battalion tactical group of 200 people, 50 instructors in Nakhichevan, 90 military advisers in Baku (they provided a liaison in the conduct of hostilities in the brigade-corps-general staff chain); 120 flight personnel at the Gabala airbase; 20 drone operators at the Dallar airfield, 50 instructors at the Yevlakh airfield, 50 instructors at the 4th Army Corps (Pirekeshkul) and 20 people at the naval base and at the Heydar Aliyev Military School in Baku. This group allegedly included 18 infantry fighting vehicles, one multiple launch rocket system, ten vehicles and up to 34 aircraft (including 6 aircraft, 8 helicopters, up to 20 drones), which provided military intelligence both in the Karabakh region and in Armenia." (*Kommersant*, "Forcing conflict, Kommersant's sources told how Turkey was preparing the ground for aggravation in Nagorno-Karabakh," November 16, 2020)

July 12–16: Tensions rise as Azerbaijan and Armenia exchange artillery fire along their borders. Twelve Azerbaijani and five Armenian soldiers are killed in the fighting. On July 16, Azerbaijani President Ilham Aliyev sacks his foreign minister, Elmar Mamedyarov, after accusing him of "meaningless negotiations" with Armenia.

August: Azerbaijan conducts large-scale military training exercises with Turkey.

September 26: Russia concludes the Kavkaz-2020 strategic exercise. "The Caucasus-2020 exercise was conducted under the leadership of the Chief of the General Staff of the Russian Armed Forces, General of the Army Valery Gerasimov, in the territory of the Southern Military District and the Black and Caspian Seas. About 80 thousand people took part in them, including employees of the Ministry of Emergency Situations and the National Guard, as well as up to 1 thousand soldiers from Armenia, Belarus, Iran, China, Myanmar and Pakistan. Up to 12.9 thousand military personnel were involved in episodes falling under the Vienna Document 2011 on Confidence- and Security-Building Measures." ("Кавказ-2020," Russian Ministry of Defense, September 27, 2020. https://function.mil.ru/news_page/country/more.htm?id=12316413@egNews)

September 27: Early on Sunday morning, major fighting erupts between Azerbaijan, Armenia and Artsakh forces along the 200-kilometer (124-mile) line of contact. Artsakh and Armenian sources report that Azerbaijan started shelling between 8:03 am to 8:10 am, and Azerbaijan reports receiving Armenian artillery and rocket fire around 6 am. Armenia said Azerbaijan's military bombed civilian settlements in Nagorno-Karabakh, including the regional capital of Stepanakert. The Azerbaijani Ministry of Defense reported that the Armenian forces fired artillery and rockets at the positions of the Azerbaijani Army "along the entire front line." In response, Armenian Prime Minister Nikol Pashinyan announces that the Azerbaijani military initiated the first attack, and that Armenia was merely responding in its own defense. In Azerbaijan, thousands of protestors "called on the government to react with greater force; after some protestors temporarily occupied Azerbaijan's parliament, protests were forcibly dispersed." (CRS Report)

Azerbaijan launches a well-planned attack against Armenian ground air defense units in Nagorno-Karabakh with the aim to gain air supremacy in the first two weeks of the war. Azerbaijan uses An-2 "Colt" biplanes, purchased from Russia, and reconfigures them as remotely piloted flying bombs to act as decoys to trip Armenian air defenses. Once the Armenians fired upon these decoys, Azerbaijani sensors (a combination of Azerbaijani satellites, aircraft and high-flying unmanned aerial vehicles) unmasked the Armenian air defense and uncovered systems were attacked by artillery, rocket forces, unmanned aerial vehicles (UAVs) and unmanned combat aerial vehicles (UCAVs). Using this method of bait, sense and strike, the Azerbaijanis are able to gain air supremacy in the first weeks of the war.

The Soviet-era OSA (NATO codename "Gecko") was the most numerous Armenian mobile air defense system in Nagorno-Karabakh. The OSA was not affective against most of the Azerbaijani UAVs. According to analysts Stijn Mitzer and Joost Oliemans, from the *Oryx* website, which chronicled every video Azerbaijan released from their precision strike systems, "Bayraktar TB2 UCAVs started releasing Roketsan MAM-L Smart Munitions over Armenian positions, striking at least three 9K33 OSA and three 9K35 STRELA-10 mobile surface-to-air missile systems. These systems appeared just as unaware and incapable of tackling the drone threat overhead as the Russian PANTSIR-S1s in Syria and Libya, and all were destroyed without ever knowing what hit them. At least twelve Armenian 9K33s were destroyed by Azerbaijani TB2s during the war." (see https://www.oryxspioenkop. com/2020/09/the-fight-for-nagorno-karabakh.html)

September 28: Armenian Prime Minister Nikol Pashinyan and Nagorno-Karabakh authorities declare martial law and military mobilization. President Erdoğan of Turkey said that Azerbaijan had to "take matters into its own hands" given the failure of international conflict resolution efforts and that Turkey would continue to support Azerbaijan "with all its resources and heart." (CRS Report) Azerbaijani forces claim to have seized Talış, a village in the Martakert Region of the Nagorno-Karabakh Republic (de facto), and the Tartar Rayon of Azerbaijan. Talış had been under Armenian control since the ceasefire in 1994 that ended the First Nagorno-Karabakh War.

September 29: Azerbaijani artillery and rocket fires, assisted by drones, destroy an Armenian column on the road from Madagiz in the direction of Aghdara. Madagis is about 68 kilometers (42 miles), and Aghdara approximately 50 kilometers (31 miles), north of the city of Stepanakert. Azerbaijani forces attack in the north and announce several towns occupied. On the same day, Armenian officials allege a Turkish F-16 fighter jet departing Azerbaijani airspace shot down an Armenian Su-25 jet in Armenian airspace. Both countries denied these reports which could not be independently verified. (CRS Report)

September 29–30: Armenia fires a surface-to-air missile at low-flying, slow-moving An-2 biplanes flying in the Nagorno-Karabakh battlespace. Sixty of these biplanes were purchased before the war and converted into remotely piloted vehicles. The intent of this conversion was to use the An-2s as bait to "turn on" the Armenian air defense system and then destroy them with swarms of loitering munitions (LMs).

Azerbaijani Chief of Defense Ministry's press service, Colonel Vagif Dargahli, reported, "… an Armenian command and observation post of the 3rd Battalion of the 1st Regiment of the Armenian army, stationed in the direction of the settlement of Hadrut of the Khojavend district was destroyed by precise fire."

October 2: The regional capital of Nagorno-Karabakh, Stepanakert, comes under heavy shelling from Azerbaijani forces.

October 3: Armenia states that heavy fighting was underway in the northern and southern directions of Nagorno-Karabakh. The Azerbaijani attacks in the north appeared to be a demonstration while the main effort of the Azerbaijani military shifted to the less mountainous districts of southern Nagorno-Karabakh where artillery, missile, and precision unmanned aerial systems (UASs) were used to target Artsakh and Armenian forces to shape the battlespace.

October 4: Fighting intensifies as Azerbaijani UASs attack Armenian air defense units in Nagorno-Karabakh while both Stepanakert and Ganja in western Azerbaijan are attacked by artillery fire. Azerbaijan announced the capture of the town of Jabrayil in southeast Nagorno-Karabakh. Jabrayil is a "ghost town," abandoned due to the fighting in the First Nagorno-Karabakh War, and lies along a critical road that leads northwest towards the town of Hadrut. Azerbaijani President Ilham Aliyev announces in a televised address, "Nagorno-Karabakh is our land. This is the end. We showed them who we are. We are chasing them like dogs." Armenian Prime Minister Pashinyan said his country was ready for "mutual concessions" with Azerbaijan.

An Armenian 9K33 OSA shoots down an Azerbaijani Sukhoi Su-25 aircraft that was targeting Armenian positions in Fuzuli. The pilot, Colonel Zaur Nudiraliye, is killed in the crash. Azerbaijani officials acknowledged the loss in December 2020. (*AMN News* (Al-Masdar Al-'Arabi—The Arab Source), 27 December, 2020)

October 5: Azerbaijan shells Stepanakert with rockets and Armenia does the same against the Azerbaijani towns of Beylagan, Barda and Tartar City. Azerbaijan reports the Armenians have withdrawn from the key town of Hadrut.

October 6: Armenia's Prime Minister Pashinyan reports that Turkey's encouragement of Azerbaijan has led to the war. Stepanakert comes under intense

Azerbaijani artillery and rocket fire. About half of the population of "The Artsakh Republic," roughly 40,000 people, are refugees and fleeing Nagorno-Karabakh. Armenia shells more Azerbaijani towns with artillery and missiles, causing casualties. Azerbaijan claims 93 civilians are killed in these strikes.

October 7: Clashes continue along the front and Azerbaijan claims to be making progress and that the Armenians are retreating to higher ground. Russian presidential spokesperson Dmitry Peskov said Russia's security commitments to Armenia via its membership in the CSTO "do not extend to Karabakh." (CRS Report) This announcement by Russia means Armenia must fight Azerbaijan alone.

October 9: Azerbaijan announces the capture of the town of Hadrut in the Khojavend District (an area in the west of Nagorno-Karabakh) and eight other villages by the Azerbaijani Army. High-resolution satellite images, from Azerbaijan's Azersky satellites, were published on the internet the day Hadrut was captured. Hadrut was a key victory for Azerbaijan, as the town is the first regional center with an Armenian population in Nagorno-Karabakh. This was also a major blow to Armenian morale. Hadrut controls a vital road into Nagorno-Karabakh and its seizure by Azerbaijan forced Armenian defenders in the Fizuli and Jabrayil regions to withdraw from their prepared positions or risk being cut-off and surrounded.

October 10: In the afternoon, Armenian forces attempt a counterattack to retake Tug, a village on the outskirts of Hadrut, but fail to retake any ground and are forced to withdraw. The Azerbaijani Ministry of Defense reported: "As a result of the clash, 38 Armenian servicemen were killed, as well as two Grad tactical missile launchers, seven artillery pieces and two trucks with ammunition were destroyed." Russia tries to broker a ceasefire, both Armenia and Azerbaijan agree, but the truce is broken almost immediately, with both sides blaming each other.

October 11: Armenian forces launch attacks on Azerbaijani units near Hadrut and Jabrayil. The attacks are repulsed.

Azerbaijani missiles and artillery strike Stepanakert as they have every day since the beginning of the war. Armenia conducts a third missile attack on the city of Ganja, in Azerbaijan. According to Azerbaijani authorities, a Scud SS-1 rocket, armed with a conventional high-explosive warhead, detonated in the city, killing seven Azerbaijani civilians.

October 12: A tweet on October 12, 2020, from the Artsakh Defense Army reported the destruction of an An-2 aircraft, used as a remotely piloted vehicle along the eastern border of Nagorno-Karabakh. The decoy biplanes preceded successful strikes by UCAVs and LMs. By mid-October, the Armenians were largely reduced to shoulder-fired air defense systems, or man-portable air defense systems, such as the SA-24 9K38 IGLA S, for protection against the Azerbaijani UAS onslaught.

Armenian Defense Ministry reports: "We Control Hadrut." According to the Armenian-based *HETQ Online* news (https://hetq.am/en/article/123000), "Armenian Ministry of Defense representative Artsrun Hovhannisyan denied earlier Azerbaijani government claims that its forces had captured the southern Artsakh town of Hadrut. Hovhannisyan, at a Goris press conference, said that efforts by special Azerbaijani guerrilla units to enter Hadrut had been repulsed and still might be in the general area surrounding the town that has some 4,000 residents."

October 14: As the missile war escalates, Azerbaijan reports it has destroyed missile launch sites in Armenia. Armenia vows to hit more targets in Azerbaijan. Azerbaijan announces Bulutan, Malikjanli, Kamartuk, Taka and Taghaser villages in the Khojavend District (an area in the southwest of Nagorno-Karabakh) were seized by the Azerbaijani Army.

October 15: The city of Stepanakert is shelled by Azerbaijani forces. Azerbaijan announces its forces have seized Arış in Fuzuli, Doşulu in Jabrayil and several more villages in Khojavend District.

In a *France 24* television interview, Azerbaijani President Aliyev denies Syrian mercenaries are fighting alongside the Azerbaijan military, stating that "no evidence was presented" to corroborate this. He also denied that the Turkish military was directly helping Azerbaijan in the conflict but did acknowledge that Turkish drones deployed by the Azerbaijani Army were "making a difference" on the ground.

October 16: Azerbaijani President Ilham Aliyev reports to news media that the Armenians were losing the war and their losses were at US$2 billion.

A video circulating on the internet appears to show Azerbaijani forces executing two captives in the town of Hadrut. An investigation by Bellingcat (an independent international collective of researchers, investigators and citizen journalists) claimed the video was genuine.

October 17: France facilitates the agreement of a new ceasefire. Azerbaijani President Aliyev announces: "… the list of the destroyed Armenian equipment includes: 234 tanks have been destroyed, 36 tanks have been taken as military booty, 49 infantry fighting vehicles have been destroyed, 24 have been taken as military booty, 16 self-propelled artillery pieces have been destroyed, 190 cannons of various calibers, two "Hurricane" systems, one TOS flame-thrower, two "Elbrus" operational tactical missile complexes, one "TOCHKA-U," 35 "OSA" anti-aircraft missile systems, three "TOR" anti-aircraft missile complexes, five "KUB" and "KRUG" anti-aircraft missile complexes, nine radio-electronic combat systems, two S-300 anti-aircraft missile systems, 196 trucks have been destroyed, and 98 have been taken as booty."

October 18: In the early morning, the ceasefire, brokered by France, is breached by both sides. Azerbaijan announces that Armenian forces fired rockets at the Azerbaijani controlled oil pipeline which connects Baku to the Russian city of Novorossiysk on the Black Sea coast. Azerbaijan further claims the rockets were destroyed by its air defense forces and the pipeline was not damaged. Armenia responded that the reports of an attack on the pipeline were false.

At 11:35 pm, Azerbaijani President Aliyev tweets that Azerbaijan has taken control of another 13 villages in the district of Jabrayil (Jrakan) in southeastern Azerbaijan near the Iranian border.

October 22: Armenian forces fire Russian-made tactical ballistic missiles at various locations inside Azerbaijan, including the city of Gabala (Azerbaijani Ministry of Foreign Affairs report). Azerbaijan forces control the border area with Iran. The town of Agbend is seized by Azerbaijani forces. Agbend is a politically sensitive location as it sits near the point at which the borders of Azerbaijan, Armenia and Iran come together.

October 23: *TRT World*, a Turkish media enterprise and strongly pro-Azerbaijani, interviews Fariz Ismailzade, the Vice Rector for External, Government and Student affairs at the ADA University in Baku, Azerbaijan. Ismailzade reported: "Azerbaijani army is very professional, organized and motivated. They fight without any foreign help, and they are eager to liberate the occupied territories. The Armenian defense line turned out to be very weak and Azerbaijani army broke it very fast. Armenian myth is gone … It is clear that Azerbaijani side is using Turkish drones and Israeli technology, and this gives them clear superiority. Armenian army has no drones and lost many tanks and other military equipment which Azerbaijani side estimated at $4.6 billion. All Armenia does so far is to launch SCUD missiles to Ganja and other towns of Azerbaijan far from the conflict area and killing kids there." From reports like this one, and a constant barrage of full-motion-videos of successful Azerbaijani drone strikes against Armenian equipment and personnel, Azerbaijan appears to be winning the information war.

Azerbaijan President Aliyev announces that the National Hero of Azerbaijan, Shukur Hamidov, was killed during operations in the Gubadli District. Hamidov was awarded the title of "Hero" in 2016 when he was in command of a battalion. It appears from casualties like this that the leaders of the Azerbaijani Army are at the front, leading their soldiers.

The Azerbaijani Army fires "Grad" rocket launchers at Lachin (Berdzor in Armenian), a key city on the main road connecting Armenia and Karabakh.

October 25: Azerbaijani claims to have seized several villages in the Zangilan (Kovsakan), Jabrayil (Jrakan) and Gubadli (Kashunik) districts as well as "part of" Kalbajar (Karvanchar) district and the city of Gubadli. These towns are in the southwest portion of disputed Nagorno-Karabakh, near or around the Lachin corridor. Armenian sources report the Azerbaijanis fired at three villages near Shusha.

Many ethnic Azeris live in northwestern Iran, and some want their region to join with Azerbaijan. Iran deployed additional military equipment and soldiers on the border with Azerbaijan and Iran. According to the Iranian news agency, tanks and other military equipment of the Islamic Revolutionary Guard Corps were deployed in the cities of Julfa, on the border with the Nakhichevan Autonomous Republic of Azerbaijan, and Khoda Afarin on the border with Azerbaijan proper "to ensure the safety of people and the border." A year after the Second Nagorno-Karabakh War ended, tensions between Azerbaijan and Iran are on the rise. See *Iran International*, "Newspaper in Tehran Sniffs Azeri-Turkish-US-Israeli Plot Against Iran," September 28, 2021.

October 26: A third ceasefire, this one brokered by the US, is broken, and the fighting continues. Armenian forces halt Azerbaijan's attack up the Lachin corridor. Sometime after this attack, the Azerbaijanis decide to delay any further armored assaults up the Lachin corridor and decide to conduct an infiltration by special forces reinforced with additional infantry support.

October 27: The Azerbaijani Army reports a UAV or LM has destroyed an Armenian S-300PS air defense missile system (NATO codename SA-10 "Grumble") deployed in Nagorno-Karabakh. The S-300 is Armenia's most sophisticated long-range surface-to-air missile system.

October 28: Armenia reports that Azerbaijan is shelling the mountain fortress town of Shusha, the second largest town in Nagorno-Karabakh.

October 29: Azerbaijani President Aliyev announces that Azerbaijani forces are 5 kilometers (3 miles) from the town of Shusha. Shusha is a largely unpopulated town with only 4,000 ethnic Armenians living there before the war. It sits on a mountainous plateau, 1,300–1,600 meters (4,265–5,250 feet) above sea level, that controls access to the vital Lachin corridor road.

Russian President Vladimir Putin said a "long-term settlement [lies] in finding a balance of interests that would suit both sides … Everyone has their own truth. There are no simple solutions, since the knot is tied in a very complicated way." (CRS Report)

In *The Daily Beast*, an American news outlet, Armenian politician and political analyst Arthur Paronyan said, "Every Armenian all across the world feels an existential threat to our nation, but nobody expects the CSTO to help. It is a dead organization." (http://www.russianinsight.com/armenia-fears-putin-isnt-coming-to-help-in-nagorno-karabakh/)

October 31–1 November: Fighting continues, and Shusha is shelled by Azerbaijani rockets and artillery. The Armenian Prime Minister Pashinyan asks Russian President Vladimir Putin for "urgent" assistance.

November 2: Armenian officials indicate 90,000 people (out of an estimated 147,000) have fled Nagorno-Karabakh due to the fighting.

Armenian sources claim they have stopped an Azerbaijani attack aimed at Shusha and destroyed one tank and several drones in the "south-eastern direction attempting to advance armored equipment to the frontline."

November 3: Azerbaijan reports its tanks firing on Armenian tanks near Khojavend, southwest of Shusha. Heavy fog and smoke from forest fires degrade UAS operations on both sides.

November 4: Azerbaijani forces occupy Dashalty, a key village just south of Shusha.

November 5: Azerbaijani special forces infiltrate Shusha from the east, south and west and occupy key defensive positions including portions of the castle.

Azerbaijan armored forces try again to push through the Lachin corridor, but the attack stalls. "Today, at 10:30 a.m., the enemy tried to launch an offensive using armored vehicles in the eastern sector. As a result of the measures taken by the Armenian side, the Azerbaijani forces were repelled leaving behind one armored vehicle, one truck, and a large number of bodies." (Armenian Ministry of Defense statement as reported by *Radio Free Europe*, https://www.rferl.org/a/fighting-over-nagorno-karabakh-continues-as-negotiations-falter/30931651.html)

At the same time, Nagorno-Karabakh authorities accuse Azerbaijan of launching artillery bombardments on civilian targets in the cities of Martuni and Shusha. No casualties were reported.

In an interview conducted on 10 November, Artsakh President Arayik Harutyunyan reported: "We ... lost control of Shushi [Shusha] on November 5, and complete control on November 7." (*HETQ Online*, published in Yerevan, Armenian, https://hetq.am/en/article/124150)

November 6: With the smoke and heavy fog, the Armenian Army is free to reinforce Shusha with tanks and armor. Heavy fighting is reported in the forests around Shusha, by Semyon Pegov, a Russian war correspondent, author of the *WarGonzo project*, who works in the conflict zone on the Armenian side (see https://youtu.be/IZcg2bJC-yQ). More Azerbaijani special forces infiltrate Shusha from the east, south, and west.

November 7: The fog partially lifts, and Azerbaijan renews UAS attacks. Armenia reports heavy and "fierce" fighting around Shusha. Armenian defense ministry spokeswoman Shushan Stepanyan reports "especially intensive and fierce combat" overnight outside Shusha and added that several Azerbaijani attacks to take the town had been defeated. Azerbaijan's Defense Ministry denied the claims. (*Kommersant*, November 8, 2020).

Armenian tanks and infantry counterattack Azerbaijani special forces. The Azerbaijani's repel every attack and several Armenian tanks are destroyed in close-quarters city fighting by Azerbaijanis firing hand-held anti-tank guided missiles. The Armenian commander in Shusha asks for artillery support from forces north of Shusha, near the capital city of Stepanakert, but is told there are only four howitzers and no ammunition. The Azerbaijanis have successfully shaped the battlefield with their UASs. By late afternoon, Shusha is largely under Azerbaijani control.

Russian journalist, Semyon Pegov, one of the few reporters who followed the war, says "The initiative passed from hand to hand—sometimes several times an hour … infiltrators and assault troops continually attack the heights and approaches to Shushi … It's really messy there. It's just darkness." Most of the Armenian defenders attempt to retreat toward Stepanakert as the sun sets.

Azerbaijani Defense reports that former Armenian Defense Minister Seyran Ohanyan's close friend was killed during the fighting in Nagorno-Karabakh. Another was seriously wounded. Their names were not disclosed. Note: former Armenian Defense Minister Colonel-General Seyran Ohanyan and his son Artur Ohanyan were seriously wounded in the fighting around Shusha on November 6.

November 8: Armenian forces continue to leave Shusha for Stepanakert. Azerbaijan claims the capture of the strategic, mountaintop town of Shusha and presses toward Stepanakert. From Shusha, Azerbaijani forces control the high ground and the approaches to the city of Stepanakert. The Armenian defenders flee toward Stepanakert with heavy casualties. Many dead Armenian soldiers were found along the road from Shusha to Stepanakert after the fighting. Armenia announces the town has not fallen and the battle is still underway. The truth is that the Azerbaijani infiltration attack seized the town and defeated the Armenians in a tough, close-combat battle.

November 9: The Azerbaijani operation to destroy the surrounded enemy forces fleeing Shusha continues. The Azerbaijani Ministry of Defense reports "On November 9, our attack UAVs destroyed one tank and one IFV [infantry fighting vehicle] of the Armenian armed forces, which attempted to attack our units in order to break out of the encirclement near the village of Zarisli on the Lachin–Shusha road." With the capture of Shusha, and the Armenians in rout, the Azerbaijanis appear concerned about the possibility of Russian intervention on Armenia's behalf. Azerbaijani forces shoot down a Russian Mi-24 helicopter inside Armenia, near Azerbaijan's Nakhichevan exclave located west of Armenia, killing two Russians and wounding one. The helicopter was reportedly escorting a Russian military convoy from Russia's 102nd military base in Gyumri, Armenia. Azerbaijan quickly issues an apology and promises an investigation into the matter. (CRS Report)

November 9–10: Armenia's military is in utter disarray and can no longer defend. Panicked civilians flee Stepanakert. Armenia acknowledges defeat. A ceasefire is declared by all sides after Armenian and Artsakh leaders agree to all Azerbaijani demands. Azerbaijani President Aliyev, Armenian Prime Minister Pashinyan and Russian President Putin issue a joint statement that several media reports referred to as a "ceasefire" or "peace agreement." The arrangement secured substantial territorial gains for Azerbaijan while retaining security for, and Armenian control over, reduced territory within Nagorno-Karabakh. The agreement officially took effect on Tuesday (November 10) at 1 am local time. (CRS Report)

November 10: Official Artsakh public address: "Artsakh President Arayik Harutyunyan, announced that they had no other choice but to agree to hand over lands to Azerbaijan in exchange for ending the war. Explaining the decision, Harutyunyan said that after 43 days of fighting, the country's armed forces had lost the regions of Fizuli, Jabrail, Kubatlu, Zangelan, the mainpublic address: part of the Hadrut region, Martuni, certain parts of the Askeran region, and the city of Shushi. The war had reached the outskirts of Stepanakert. Had the fighting continued at the same pace, they would have lost the whole of Artsakh in a matter of days, leaving many victims.

Armenian Prime Minister Pashinyan announces trilateral negotiations with Azerbaijan and Russia produced a ceasefire that surrendered most of Nagorno-Karabakh to Azerbaijan. For Armenia, it was a de facto surrender; for Azerbaijan, a decisive military and political victory; for Russia, a dangerous change in the status quo that strengthened Russia's hand with Armenia but exposed the South Caucasus region to Turkey; and for Turkey it was a resounding military and geopolitical success, and a boon to the Turkish arms, and particularly UAS, industry. Russia announces it will send 2,000 troops to monitor the ceasefire. When they arrive on November 11, they find a grizzly scene of dead Armenians on the sides of the road from Stepanakert to Shusha. Russian forces move into Nagorno-Karabakh. Throughout the war, Russia sat on the sidelines.

Losses: Armenia's losses have been staggering for such a small country. In 44 days, it has lost 250 tanks (144 destroyed, 5 damaged, and 101 captured), mostly to Azerbaijani UASs and LMs. A precise listing of Armenia's and Azerbaijan's losses were cataloged by *Oryx*, operated independently by Stijn Mitzer, at https://www.oryxspioenkop.com/2020/09/the-fight-for-nagorno-karabakh.html. Each of the vehicles listed has a photograph taken from a UAS, LM or electro-optical-outfitted anti-tank guided missile.

November 16: At least 300 bodies of Armenian soldiers are removed from Shusha. Russian news outlet *Kommersant* records that "the number of flights of Turkey's military transport aviation to Azerbaijan (mainly in transit through Georgia) increased sharply" from September to November, providing Azerbaijan with military supplies, and claimed Turkey "deliberately planned and provoked" the Second Nagorno-Karabakh War.

Changes Must be Made Swiftly

"I'm not convinced that we have fully thought our way through all of the challenges we may face on the future high-end battlefield if deterrence fails. We need to look harder at key cases, such as the Nagorno-Karabakh war between Armenia and Azerbaijan... Perhaps hardest of all, these changes must be made swiftly."

Secretary of the Army Secretary Christine Wormuth, October 11, 2021

Questions for Further Study

Questions Concerning the Changing Methods of Warfare Introduced by the Deployment of Long-Range Precision Fires, Ubiquitous Sensors, UCAV, UAS, and LMs

Asking the Right Questions is the Beginning of Wisdom

1. In a future conflict, if the enemy moves first, and is equipped with systems similar to those used in 2020's Second Nagorno-Karabakh War, they will have a tremendous advantage. How does a modern military counter the enemy's first-move advantage?

2. In military formations, who oversees the counter unmanned aerial system (CUAS) and loitering munitions (LM) fight? Who is responsible for winning the fight at various echelons of command such as corps, division, brigade, and battalion?

3. Is training keeping up with the ever-changing methods of war. Are military units conducting wargames, at multiple echelons, across the full spectrum of the force, to learn from the current battlespace threats?

4. If unmanned combat aerial vehicles (UCAVs) and loitering munitions proved themselves as weapons of modern war in the Second Nagorno-Karabakh War, how should these systems be organized into current military units? Should UCAVs and LMs be controlled by the artillery, air defense, maneuver elements, or all the above?

5. Protecting friendly forces from UCAV, LM, and unmanned aerial system (UAS) attack is vital. Since there are no ethical issues with machines destroying machines, should human out of the loop CUAS systems, designed to operate autonomously under electronic countermeasures and

with the full loss of satellite navigation signals, be used to automatically hunt down and destroy enemy UASs?

6. Should militaries develop smart anti-tank mines, such as the top-attack XM204, that are moveable/mobile autonomous anti-tank systems? See Joseph Trevithick, "The Army Wants Networked Mines That Leap Up To Attack The Tops Of Tanks," *The Warzone*, https://www.thedrive.com/the-war-zone/40080/the-army-wants-networked-mines-that-leap-up-to-attack-the-tops-of-tanks

7. Can we fight in a transparent battlespace without masking our forces? Masking is the full-spectrum, multi-domain effort to deceive enemy sensors and disrupt enemy targeting. What can we do today to mask forces in a transparent battlespace?

8. The most effective LMs, such as the Harop, use sophisticated electro-optical systems for autonomous targeting. What can be done to fool computer vision systems to miss their intended targets?

9. How can a military force use robotic systems as decoys and to thicken formations with fire and logistical support?

10. How can a military force increase the survivability of large, pop-up tent command posts in a battlespace influenced by LMs and UASs?

11. If C5ISR (Command, Control, Computers, Communications, Cyber, Intelligence, Surveillance, and Reconnaissance) must be re-imagined to survive and execute mission command in the modern battlespace, how do we protect these assets? Do we need to re-imagine our C5ISR configurations, systems, and organizational structures?

12. How does a commander conduct mission command and conduct cross-domain maneuver if LMs and UASs are hunting command posts?

13. Does mission command training need to adapt to meet current battlespace capabilities?

14. How does a modern military force protect Combat Support and Combat Service Support, and protect and maintain its ability to conduct combat support and logistics in the modern battlespace influenced by long-range precision fires, UASs and LMs?

Bibliography and Further Reading

Allen, T.S.; Askonas, Jonathan; and Brown, Kyle, "How The Army Out-Innovated the Islamic State's Drones," December 21, 2020. 2020, https://warontherocks.com/2020/12/how-the-army-out-innovated-the-islamic-states-drones/

Antal, John, "Top Attack: Lessons Learned from the Second Nagorno-Karabakh War," US Army Training and Doctrine Command, *Mad Scientist Podcast 317*, April 1, 2021, https://madsciblog.tradoc.army.mil/317-top-attack-lessons-learned-from-the-second-nagorno-karabakh-war/

Atherton, Kelsey, "Russia's Carnivora is designed for a drone-eat-drone world," *C4ISR.net*, December 13, 2019, https://www.c4isrnet.com/unmanned/2018/12/14/russias-carnivora-is-designed-for-a-drone-eat-drone-world/

Barno, David, and Bensahel, Nora, "The Drone Beats of War: The US Vulnerability to Targeted Killings," January 21, 2020, https://warontherocks.com/2020/01/the-drone-beats-of-war-the-u-s-vulnerability-to-targeted-killings/

Bendett, Samuel, "Russia's real-world experience is driving counter-drone innovations," *Defense News*, May 23, 2021, https://www.defensenews.com/opinion/commentary/2021/05/23/russias-real-world-experience-is-driving-counter-drone-innovations/

Bryen, Stephen, "Armed drones revolutionizing the future of war, UAVs were decisive in Azerbaijan's recent defeat of Armenia and global militaries have taken note of lessons learned," December 9, 2020, https://asiatimes.com/2020/12/armed-drones-revolutionizing-the-future-of-war/

Eckel, Mike, "Drone Wars: In Nagorno-Karabakh, The Future Of Warfare Is Now," *Radio Free Europe*, October 9, 2020, https://www.rferl.org/a/drone-wars-in-nagorno-karabakh-the-future-of-warfare-is-now/30885007.html

Ho, Ben, "Takeaways for Singapore's Ground-Based Air Defense," *Journal of Indo-Pacific Affairs* August 25, 2021, https://www.airuniversity.af.edu/JIPA/Display/Article/2743721/the-second-nagorno-karabakh-war-takeaways-for-singapores-ground-based-air-defen/#sdendnote21sym

Kofman, Michael, "A Look at the Military Lessons of the Nagorno-Karabakh Conflict," December 14, 2020, https://www.russiamatters.org/analysis/look-military-lessons-nagorno-karabakh-conflict

Kurç, Dr. Çağlar, "The Second Nagorno-Karabakh War and UCAVs," Centre for Strategic Research and Analysis International Report Vol. 7 No. 3., Jul–Sep 2021, https://politicalreflectionmagazine.com/wp-content/uploads/2021/07/PR_Issue28_A4.pdf

Lee, Rob and Michael Kofman and Jack Watling, "The Nagorno-Karabakh Conflict: A Reflection on Modern Warfare," podcast, https://www.fpri.org/multimedia/2020/10/the-nagorno-karabakh-conflict-a-reflection-on-modern-warfare/

Mazza, Michael, "Defending Taiwan: Lessons from the 2020 Nagorno-Karabakh War," December 2, 2020, https://

Mitzer, Stijn, and Olieman, Joost, (in collaboration with Jakub Janovsky, Dan, and COIN), "Documenting Losses On The Sides Of Armenia And Azerbaijan," *Oryx*, Sunday, September 27, 2020, https://www.oryxspioenkop.com/2020/09/the-fight-for-nagorno-karabakh.html

Protopapas, Georgios, "Drones win Wars—Message to Greece," December 20, 2020, https://greekcitytimes.com/2020/12/20/caucasus-drones-greece/

Rumbaugh, Wes and Shaikh, Shaan, "The Air and Missile War in Nagorno-Karabakh: Lessons for the Future of Strike and Defense," December 8, 2020, https://www.csis.org/analysis/air-and-missile-war-nagorno-karabakh-lessons-future-strike-and-defense

Sovetkin, Sergey, "Nagorno-Karabakh. Each Side's Tactics," *Military Review* (Russian), October 5, 2020, https://topwar.ru/175785-taktika-po-video.html

Spencer, John, and Harshana Ghoorhoo, "The Battle of Shusha City and the Missed Lessons of the 2020 Nagorno-Karabakh War," July 16, 2021, https://azerfocus.com/the-battle-of-shusha-city-and-the-missed-lessons-of-the-2020-nagorno-karabakh-war/

Urcosta, Ridivan Bari, "Drones in the Nagornoa-Karabakh War," *Small Wars Journal*, October 23, 2020, https://smallwarsjournal.com/jrnl/art/drones-nagorno-karabakh

Watling, Jack, "The Key to Armenia's Tank Losses: The Sensors, Not the Shooters," *RUSI Defense Systems*, 6 October 2020, https://rusi.org/publication/rusi-defence-systems/key-armenia-tank-losses-sensors-not-shooters

Watling, Jack and Kaushal, Sidharth, "The Democratization of Precision Strike in the Nagorno-Karabakh Conflict," 22 October 2020, https://rusi.org/commentary/democratisation-precision-strike-nagorno-karabakh-conflict

Yermakov, Alexander, "Unmanned Aerial Vehicles over Nagorno-Karabakh: Revolution or Another Day of Battle," Vladivostok, Far Eastern Federal University, December 4, 2020, https://valdaiclub.com/a/highlights/unmanned-aerial-vehicles-over-nagorno-karabakh/?sphraseid=1280336

About the Author

John F. Antal, Colonel, USA (Retired)

Soldier, Author, Speaker, Leadership Development Coach, Journalist, Technologist, Strategist and Futurist

In 2021, John lectured extensively on the lessons learned from the Second Nagorno-Karabakh War. In 2020–2021, John conducted a deep study of the Second Nagorno-Karabakh War and made more than 55 separate presentations to senior US and allied military and government officials on the lessons learned from the war. He was also featured on the Army Futures Command *Mad Scientist* Podcast, "Top Attack: Lessons Learned from the Second Nagorno-Karabakh War" in April 2021, the US Army Training and Doctrine Command's "Knowledge Management at War—Lessons from Nagorno-Karabakh" video in May 2021, and the Fires Center of Excellence presentation on the "Military Lessons of the Second Nagorno-Karabakh War" on September 2, 2021.

John is an award-winning author of 16 books and hundreds of magazine articles about leadership, history, and war. He is a journalist and has been a successful magazine editor. He is a frequent contributor to radio, podcast, and television shows concerning leadership, current military events, and the art of war. His previous book, *Leadership Rising* (published in the second half of 2021), is a leadership primer for emerging and experienced leaders.

John's military experience spans 30 years in the US Army as an armor and cavalry officer. He is a graduate of the United States Military Academy at West Point, an Airborne Ranger, earned the Expert Infantryman's Badge, and is a distinguished graduate of the US Army Command and General Staff College and the Army War College. He has commanded combat units from platoon through regiment and served on division, corps, and multinational staff. He served in the Pentagon as Special Assistant to the Chairman of the Joint Chiefs of Staff; commanded the 16th Cavalry Regiment at Fort Knox, Kentucky;

and served as the G3, Operations Officer, for III Armored Corps, Fort Hood, Texas. In recent years, John has served on the US Army Science Board.

After retiring from the US Army in 2003, he was hired by Microsoft Games Studios to develop an interactive entertainment company in Texas. In his 15 years in the video game industry, he has led technology development teams to create successful multi-million dollar, AAA+ video game titles.

John speaks across the nation about leadership and raises the leadership awareness of individual, teams, and companies. As a leadership consultant, he teaches leadership to private, corporate and government groups.

John Antal's purpose in life is to "develop leaders and inspire service." What is your purpose in life?

You can contact John at American-Leadership.com

Endnotes

Chapter 1

1   Carl Von Clausewitz, edited and translated by Michael Howard and Peter Paret, *On War* (Princeton University Press, Princeton, New Jersey), 1989, p. 87.

2   Department of the Army, *Mountain Operations, FM 3-97.6*, Washington, DC, November 28, 2000, pp. 4–25.

3   Department of the Army, *Mountain Operations, FM 3-97.6*, Washington, DC, November 28, 2000, pp. 4–25.

4   Jo Laycock, "Nagorno-Karabakh's Myth of Ancient Hatreds," *History Today*, October 8, 2020, https://www.historytoday.com/miscellanies/nagorno-karabakhs-myth-ancient-hatreds

5   International Crisis Group, Nagorno-Karabakh: Viewing the Conflict from the Ground, Europe Report N°166, p. 1 – 14 September 2005, https://d2071andvip0wj.cloudfront.net/166-nagorno-karabakh-viewing-the-conflict-from-the-ground.pdf

6   Azerbaijan and Armenia: The Nagorno-Karabakh Conflict, Congressional Research Service, January 7, 2021, p. 3. https://crsreports.congress.gov

7   Hans-Joachim Schmidt, The Four-Day War Has Diminished the Chances of Peace in Nagorno-Karabakh," *OSCE Yearbook 2016*, Baden-Baden 2017, p. 115. https://www.hsfk.de/publikationen/publikationssuche/publikation/the-four-day-war-has-diminshed-the-chances-of-peace-in-nagorno-karabakh/

8   Benjamin Brimelow, "Turkey is building new ships, tanks, and missiles to boost its military and send a message to the rest of NATO," *Business Insider*, August 6, 2021, https://www.businessinsider.com/turkey-is-modernizing-its-military-to-send-message-to-nato-2021-8?op=1

9   Paul Iddon, "The Growing Military Cooperation Between Turkey And Azerbaijan," *Forbes*, July 27, 2021, https://www.forbes.com/sites/pauliddon/2021/07/27/the-growing-military-cooperation-between-turkey-and-azerbaijan/

10 Schmidt, "The Four-Day War Has Diminished the Chances of Peace in Nagorno-Karabakh," pp. 111–123. https://ifsh.de/file/publication/OSCE_Yearbook_en/2016/Schmidt-en.pdf

11 *Vz.ru*: "The Azerbaijani Army Is Being Purged Of The Officers And Generals Who Started Their Career In The Soviet Union ... Those Who Have Completed ... Training In Turkey Are Placed In Key Positions – Turkish Advisers Are Placed Above Them," https://www.memri.org/reports/russian-media-outlet-vzru-azerbaijani-army-being-purged-officers-and-generals-who-started

12 Staff Writer, "Muscle flexing: Why Azerbaijan is Conducting Exercises with Turkey: Azerbaijan and Turkey Hold Joint Military Exercises Since 29 July," *Gazeta.Ru*, 28 July 2020. https://www.gazeta.ru/politics/2020/07/28_a_13168861.shtml?updated

Chapter 2

1   The TOS-1 is a Soviet-era, Russian-made, 220mm, 30-barrel or 24-barrel multiple rocket launcher system that launches thermobaric munitions. It is mounted on a T-72 tank chassis. TOS-1 was designed to attack enemy fortified positions, troops in open country, and lightly armored vehicles and transports.

2   Sergey Sovetkin, "Nagorno-Karabakh, the Tactics of Both Sides," *Russian Military Review* journal, October 5, 2020, https://topwar.ru/175785-taktika-po-video.html

3   "War in Nagorno-Karabakh – 2020, Military Analysis," November 25, 2020, https://www.wardiary.net/

4   For more information on Turkish–Azerbaijani cooperation and planning of the Second Nagorno-Karabakh War see: Haldun Yalçınkaya, "Turkey's Overlooked Role in the Second Nagorno-Karabakh War," January 21, 2021, https://www.gmfus.org/news/turkeys-overlooked-role-second-nagorno-karabakh-war

5   A. V. Lavrov, "44-Days of the Second Karabakh War," In *Storm in the Caucasus,* Center for Analysis of Strategies and Technologies, Moscow R. N. Pukhova, editor, p. 44, 2021, cast.ru/books/burya-na-kavkaze.html

6   *Vz.ru,* "Those Trained in Turkey are Placed in Key Positions – Turkish Advisers Are Placed Above Them," https://www.memri.org/reports/russian-media-outlet-vzru-azerbaijani-army-being-purged-officers-and-generals-who-started

7   Eric Chan, "What Taiwan's Military Can Learn From the Armenia-Azerbaijan War," *The Diplomat,* December 9, 2020, https://thediplomat.com/2020/12/what-taiwans-military-can-learn-from-the-armenia-azerbaijan-war/

8   Stijn Mitzer and Joost Oliemans, "Aftermath: Lessons Of The Nagorno-Karabakh War Are Paraded Through The Streets Of Baku," *Oryx,* January 26, 2021, https://www.oryxspioenkop.com/2021/01/aftermath-lessons-of-nagorno-karabakh.html

9   The 9K33 OSA is highly mobile, low-altitude, short-range tactical surface-to-air missile system developed in the Soviet Union in the 1960s and fielded in 1972. Its export version name is "Romb."

10 Mitzer and Oliemans, "Aftermath: Lessons Of The Nagorno-Karabakh War Are Paraded Through The Streets Of Baku."

11 "Turkish Air Force Used E-7A Peace Eagle To Hunt And Destroy S-300 Using TB2 Drones," *Global Defense Corp,* November 7, 2020, https://www.globaldefensecorp.com/2020/11/07/turkish-air-force-used-e-7a-peace-eagle-to-find-and-destroy-s-300-using-tb2-drones/

12 Dmitry Shlapentokh, "Nagorno-Karabakh War and Russia's Pursuit of Gas Interests," Institute of Modern Russia, IMR, February 2, 2021.

13 *World Directory of Modern Military Aircraft,* Azerbaijan Air Force (2021) https://www.wdmma.org/armenian-air-force.php

14 Ibid.

15 Mitzer and Oliemans, "Aftermath: Lessons Of The Nagorno-Karabakh War Are Paraded Through The Streets Of Baku."

16 Jack Watling, "Nagorno-Karabakh: The Democratization of Precision Strike and the Viability of Military Power," *Central Asia-Caucasus Analyst,* March 25, 2021, https://cacianalyst.org/publications/analytical-articles/item/13665-nagorno-karabakh-the-democratization-of-precision-strike-and-the-viability-of-military-power.html

17 "Results of a two-day standoff on April 2-5th, 2016," *Vestnik Kavkaza,* in Russian, 2016, https://vestnikkavkaza.net/articles/Results-of-a-two-day-standoff-on-April-2-5th.html

18 Can Kasapoglu as quoted in an article by Ron Synovitz, "Technology, Tactics, And Turkish Advice Lead Azerbaijan To Victory In Nagorno-Karabakh," *Radio Free Europe*, November 13, 2020, https://www.rferl.org/a/technology-tactics-and-turkish-advice-lead-azerbaijan-to-victory-in-nagorno-karabakh/30949158.html

19 Chan, "What Taiwan's Military Can Learn From the Armenia-Azerbaijan War."

20 "President Aliyev named some of Armenian equipment destroyed, taken as booty in recent days," October 17, 2020, https://en.trend.az/azerbaijan/politics/3318691.html

21 Mike Dahm, "The Reality of War Should Define Information Warfare," *US Naval Institute Proceedings* Vol. 147/3/1, 417, March 2021.

22 Ophelia Simonyan, "The Weapon of Information in the Second Karabakh War. Yerevan's Take," *JAMnews*, Go Group Media, April 17, 2021, https://jam-news.net/the-weapon-of-information-in-the-second-karabakh-war-yerevans-take/

23 Maedeh Sharifi, "How State-led Disinformation Fuels the Nagorno-Karabakh Conflict," TRT World, October 23, 2021. https://www.trtworld.com/magazine/how-state-led-disinformation-fuels-the-nagorno-karabakh-conflict-40841

24 Can Kasapoglu as quoted in an article by Ron Synovitz, "Technology, Tactics, And Turkish Advice Lead Azerbaijan To Victory In Nagorno-Karabakh."

25 Stijn Mitzer and Joost Oliemans, "The Fight For Nagorno-Karabakh: Documenting Losses On The Sides Of Armenia And Azerbaijan," September 27, 2020, https://www.oryxspioenkop.com/2020/09/the-fight-for-nagorno-karabakh.html

26 A decisive point is geographic place, specific key event, critical factor, or function that, when acted upon, allows commanders to gain a marked advantage over an adversary or contribute materially to achieving success. The definition of a Center of Gravity is "the source of power that provides moral or physical strength, freedom of action, or will to act." Thus, the center of gravity is usually seen as the "source of strength."

27 The SandCat is a 4x4, wheeled composite-armored vehicle based on a commercial Ford F-Series truck chassis and manufactured by Israeli based Plasan Sasa Ltd, see https://www.plasan.com/wp-content/uploads/2017/06/Plasan-SandCat-ENG.pdf

28 Tarafından Yayınlandı, "What About the Environment in Karabakh?," Turkish Energy Strategies and Policy Research Center (TESPAM), July 8, 2021, https://www.tespam.org/what-about-the-environment-in-karabakh-2/

29 John Spencer and Harshana Ghoorhoo, "The Battle of Shusha City and the Missed Lessons of the 2020 Nagorno-Karabakh War," *Azerbaijan Focus*, July 16, 2021, https://azerfocus.com/the-battle-of-shusha-city-and-the-missed-lessons-of-the-2020-nagorno-karabakh-war/

30 "We went to Shusha through Armenians, they didn't know," *Qafqazinfo.az* online newspaper, December 3, 2020, https://qafqazinfo.az/news/detail/susaya-ermenilerin-icinden-kecib-getdik-xeberleri-olmadi-xtd-zabitivideo-307243

31 Spencer and Ghoorhoo, "The Battle of Shusha City and the Missed Lessons of the 2020 Nagorno-Karabakh War."

32 Samvel Babayan, "Failed operations, lack of weapons, refusal of orders, Samvel Babayan's revelations from the 44-day war," *CivilNet*, in Armenian, December 13, 2020, https://www.civilnet.am/news/472441/

33 Spencer and Ghoorhoo, "The Battle of Shusha City and the Missed Lessons of the 2020 Nagorno-Karabakh War."

34 Gohar Hakobyan, "Arayik Harutyunyan: 'If military operations continued, we would have lost all of Artsakh,'" *Aravot–Armenian News*, November 10, 2020, https://www.aravot-en.am/2020/11/10/270024/

35 Spencer and Ghoorhoo, "The Battle of Shusha City and the Missed Lessons of the 2020 Nagorno-Karabakh War.

36 Azerbaijani President Ilham Aliyev, "We have destroyed enemy in hand-to-hand battle, crossing ravines, forests, mountains, and liberated Shusha," *Trend Azerbaijani News*, November 24, 2020.

37 Maria Titizian, editor in chief, "War Ends, What Follows?," *EVN*, November 10, 2020, https://www.evnreport.com/spotlight-karabakh/war-ends-what-next-live-updates

38 Wojciech Górecki, "Nagorno-Karabakh: Armenia's Surrender, Russia's Success," https://www.osw.waw.pl/en/publikacje/analizy/2020-11-10/nagorno-karabakh-armenias-surrender-russias-success

39 Jack Losh, "Russian Troops in Nagorno-Karabakh 'Clearly a Win for Moscow'," *Foreign Policy*, November 25, 2020, https://foreignpolicy.com/2020/11/25/russian-troops-nagorno-karabakh-peacekeepers-win-moscow-armenia-azerbaijan/

Chapter 3

1 Burak Bekdil, "The Rise and Rise of Turkish Drone Technology," Begin-Sadat Center for Strategic Studies, April 11, 2021, https://besacenter.org/the-rise-and-rise-of-turkish-drone-technology/, and Baykar's website at https://baykardefence.com/

2 See "Harop Loitering Munitions UCAV System," *AirForce Technology* newsletter, https://www.airforce-technology.com/projects/haroploiteringmuniti/

3 See YouTube, "Turkish Unveils New Version of Bayraktar TB2S Satellite UCAV," *Public Defense*, November 11, 2020, https://youtu.be/gy9Fr8d9Ze4

4 The fuel–air explosive is one of the best-known types of thermobaric weapon.

5 Asian Military Review, "Roketsan's Smart Munitions for Low Payload Platforms," December 6, 2018 https://www.asianmilitaryreview.com/2018/12/roketsans-smart-munitions-for-low-payload-platforms/

6 Israel Aerospace Industries (IAI), Harop Loitering Munition, https://www.iai.co.il/p/harop

7 See https://cp-aeronautics.com/wp-content/uploads/2019/11/Orbiter-1k.pdf

Chapter 5

1 DefenseWorld.Net, "Russia's $42M EW System did not Work in Nagorno-Karabakh: Armenian PM Complains," December 9, 2020. https://www.defenseworld.net/news/28502/Russia___s__42M_EW_System_did_not_Work_in_Nagorno_Karabakh__Armenian_PM_Complains#.YZu8lvHMKw5

Chapter 6

1 Clean Energy Institute, University of Washington, "What is a Lithium-ion Battery and How Does it Work?" 2020. https://www.cei.washington.edu/education/science-of-solar/battery-technology/

2 Steve Hanley, "Here's Everything We Know About The Tesla Battery Patent Filed Last Week." (CleanTechnica), May 10, 2020. https://cleantechnica.com/2020/05/10/heres-everything-we-know-about-the-tesla-battery-patent-filed-last-week/

Chapter 8

1   Heinz Guderian, *Achtung-Panzer! The Development of Armoured Forces, Their Tactics and Operational Potential* (first printed in Stutgart in 1937), reprinted Arms & Armour; May 1, 1993), p. 357.
2   See https://www.youtube.com/watch?v=4SFBK6yRjro)

Chapter 9

1   Ed Stacey, "Future Warfighting in the 2030s: An Interview with Franz-Stefan Gady," *Strife*, King's College London, Department of War Studies, September 9, 2020, https://www.strifeblog.org/2020/09/09/future-warfighting-in-the-2030s-an-interview-with-franz-stefan-gady/
2   Lester W. Grau and Charles K. Bartles, "The Russian Reconnaissance Fire Complex Comes of Age," University of Oxford, Changing Charaacter of War Center, May 30, 2018. https://www.ccw.ox.ac.uk/blog/2018/5/30/the-russian-reconnaissance-fire-complex-comes-of-age
3   See Fibrotex, https://www.fibrotex-tech.com/fibrotex-usa-selected-deliver-us-armys-next-generation-camouflage-system-0
4   Sergey Ptichkin, "New aerosol ammunition adopted by the Russian army," *RG.RU*, September 17, 2021, https://rg.ru/2021/09/17/novyj-aerozolnyj-boepripas-priniat-na-vooruzhenie-rossijskoj-armii.html
5   Aleksey Ivanov, "Electromagnetic bombs have been created in Russia," *RG.RU*, September 29, 2017, https://rg.ru/2017/09/28/v-rossii-sozdali-svch-bomby.html
6   Alon Gorodetsky and Chengyi Xu , "Adaptive Infrared-reflecting Systems Inspired by Cephalopods," EuropePMC.org, March 1, 2018. https://europepmc.org/article/MED/29599237
7   BAE Systems plc (BAE), "ADAPTIV—Cloak of Invisibility," BAE Systems.com, 2021. https://www.baesystems.com/en/feature/adativ-cloak-of-invisibility
8   Michio Kaku. *Physics of the Impossible : a Scientific Exploration into the World of Phasers, Force Fields, Teleportation, and Time Travel,* New York :Doubleday, 2008. p.22.

Chapter 10

1   Vasiliy G. Reznichenko, Ivan N. Vorobyev, and Nickolay F. Miroshnichenko, *Tactics* (Moscow: Voyenizdat, 1987), trans. Foreign Broadcast Information Service (FBIS), JPRS-UMA-88-008-L-1, June 29, 1988, pp.8-9 and 114. https://ia803103.us.archive.org/12/items/DTIC_ADA183185/DTIC_ADA183185.pdf
2   Dr. Al Emondi, "Next-Generation Nonsurgical Neurotechnology," Defense Advanced Research Projects, darpa.mil, 2021. https://www.darpa.mil/program/next-generation-nonsurgical-neurotechnology
3   See the video at https://youtu.be/DVvmgjBL74w

Chapter 11

1   Carl Von Clausewitz, Michael Howard, and Peter Paret. *On War.* Princeton, N.J.: Princeton University Press., 1976. p. 695. Note: Clausewitz explains, "The principal question... is,

whether the resistance which is intended by the defense of mountains is to be relative or absolute—whether it is only intended to last for a time or is meant to end in a decisive victory. For a resistance of the first kind mountainous ground is in a high degree suitable and introduces into it a very powerful element of strength; for one of the latter kind, on the contrary, it is in general not at all suitable, or only so in some special cases."

2   Gen Sir Mark Carleton-Smith, as reported by Andrew White, "DSEI 2021: CGS Underlines Changing Nature of Warfare," Shephard Press Limited, 33 St James's Square London, SW1Y 4JS. September 16, 2021. https://www.shephardmedia.com/news/defence-notes/dsei-2021-cgs-underlines-changing-nature-warfare/

3   General Vladimir Slipchenko, *Non-Contact Wars*. Moscow: January 1, 2000.

4   Oleg Vladykin, "In the West of the Country, Rocket and Artillerymen Became More Active," Nezavisimaya Gazeta, February 17, 2017. In Russian: На западе страны активизировались ракетчики и артиллеристы https://nvo.ng.ru/nvoevents/2017-02-17/2_937_news.html

5   People's Liberation Army of China Academy of Military Science Military Strategy Dept. trans, China Aerospace Studies Institute. *In Their Own Words: Foreign Military Thought, Science of Military Strategy (2013)*, (Air University, 55 Lemay Plaza, Montgomery, AL 36112), p. 161. https://www.airuniversity.af.edu/Portals/10/CASI/documents/Translations/2021-02-08%20Chinese%20Military%20Thoughts-%

6   Note: A kill chain represents how an attack is structured and consists of target identification, dispatching a force to engage the target, deciding to attack the target, and then engaging the target.

7   Stijn Mitzer and Joost Oliemans, "Aftermath: Lessons Of The Nagorno-Karabakh War Are Paraded Through The Streets Of Baku," *Oryx*, January 26, 2021. https://www.oryxspioenkop.com/2021/01/aftermath-lessons-of-nagorno-karabakh.html.

8   Ibrahim Altay, editor in chief. "Turkish Drone Magnate Baykar Inks 13th Export Deal," *Daily Sabah*, Istanbul, October 28,2021. https://www.dailysabah.com/business/defense/turkish-drone-magnate-baykar-inks-13th-export-deal

9   Elisabetta Confaloneiri, "The Turkish Bayraktar TB2: Ankara's Renewed Prominence in the Drone Market," European Army Interoperability Centre. August 5, 2021.

10 For more information on the Harop, see: https://www.iai.co.il/p/harop

11 For more information on the Orbiter, see: https://aeronautics-sys.com/wp-content/themes/aeronautics/pdf/orbiter_1k_v2.pdf

12 Amar Diwakar, in an interview with Abishur Prakash, "The Future of War and Deterrence in an Age of Autonomous Weapons," *TRT World* (Turkish Radio and Television Corporation). June 17, 2021. https://www.trtworld.com/magazine/the-future-of-war-and-deterrence-in-an-age-of-autonomous-weapons-47602

13 Joint Staff J7, "Insights and Best Practices Focus Paper on "Mission Command," (Department of Defense, Second Edition. Deployable Training Division (DTD) J7, Deputy Director for Joint Training, Suffolk, VA), January 2020. https://www.jcs.mil/Portals/36/Documents/Doctrine/fp/missioncommand_fp_2nd_ed.pdf?ver=2020-01-13-083451-207.

14 Charles Bartles, "Russian Loitering Munitions to Enter Serial Production for Domestic and Export Markets," OEW Online, October 30, 2021. https://oew-online.com/?p=3292

Index